6 SECRETS TO STARTUP SUCCESS

How to Turn Your Entrepreneurial
Passion into a Thriving Business

JOHN BRADBERRY

Foreword by Pamela Slim,
author of *Escape from Cubicle Nation*

ⒶMACOM

AMERICAN MANAGEMENT ASSOCIATION
New York • Atlanta • Brussels • Chicago • Mexico City • San Francisco
Shanghai • Tokyo • Toronto • Washington, D.C.

This publication is designed to provide accurate and authoritative information in regard to the subject matter covered. It is sold with the understanding that the publisher is not engaged in rendering legal, accounting, or other professional service. If legal advice or other expert assistance is required, the services of a competent professional person should be sought.

Library of Congress Cataloging-in-Publication Data
Bradberry, John, 1961–
   6 secrets to startup success : how to turn your entrepreneurial passion into a thriving business / John Bradberry ; foreword by Pamela Slim.
      p. cm.
   Includes bibliographical references and index.
   ISBN-13: 978-0-8144-1606-8 (hardcover)
   ISBN-10: 0-8144-1606-3 (hardcover)
   1. New business enterprises—Management. 2. Entrepreneurship. 3. Success in business. I. Title. II. Title: Six secrets to startup success.
   HD62.5.B723 2011
   658.1'1—dc22
                                    2010039039

About AMA

American Management Association (www.amanet.org) is a world leader in talent development, advancing the skills of individuals to drive business success. Our mission is to support the goals of individuals and organizations through a complete range of products and services, including classroom and virtual seminars, webcasts, webinars, podcasts, conferences, corporate and government solutions, business books, and research. AMA's approach to improving performance combines experiential learning—learning through doing—with opportunities for ongoing professional growth at every step of one's career journey.

Printing Number

10   9   8   7   6   5   4   3   2

CONTENTS

Foreword

Most of us harbor thoughts of starting a business.

It is a delicious fantasy while staring at gray cubicle walls, or toiling outside for an hourly wage under the command of someone who is profiting from the fruits of your labor.

"I can do this," you say, "How hard could it be?"

Some, emboldened by the desire to take charge of their own destiny, actually take the leap.

Things can go well for a while, until the moment when they realize that there are a whole lot of things that can go wrong.

And that if they had known then what they knew now, they may not have been so quick to give notice at their job, or to invest precious money, time, and energy in an idea that was not quite ready for prime time.

The greatest heartbreak, popular success publications tout, is failing to do something about your burning passion for a world-changing idea.

A greater heartbreak, in reality, is placing this idea onto a shaky foundation, and watching it fall apart.

What is really driving your desire to start a business? If you are like most people:

- You want to make an impact in the world.

- You want to create wealth for yourself and your family.

- You want to translate your idea into a tangible product or service.

- You want to have flexibility to spend time with your family.

- You want to feel fully alive.

- You want to use your strengths in a way that leads to deep value.

These desires are not fantasies. There are thousands of entrepreneurs who have built successful businesses on a solid foundation and accomplish these goals every day.

The difference between them and others who end up in the "failed" pile of startup statistics is that they cared enough about their ideas to give them the very best chance to succeed.

Caring means researching. Caring means testing ideas before committing too many resources. Caring means not brushing off people who challenge your idea. Caring means getting the very best advice from people who have successfully guided companies through the startup phase and beyond.

In *6 Secrets to Startup Success,* John Bradberry, a calm, steady hand and seasoned mentor, brings an invaluable voice of reason that will guide you every step of the way without preaching or dampening your enthusiasm. He celebrates entrepreneurial passion while giving it the structure it needs to result in business success:

> The solution lies not in ratcheting down passion, but in elevating awareness. By pausing early in your startup process to take an objective look at yourself and what you bring to the table—your purpose, goals, skills, resources, and needs—you can develop a highly valuable kind of optimism, one that rests on the rock of clear, honest assessment and willful preparation. I call it *earned optimism.*

It is such a relief to know that sustained energy to grow your business is not based on manufactured enthusiasm or pep talks from motivational speakers. It is based on executing a well-defined yet flexible plan in tiny steps, leaning into the market and adjusting your business model as you go.

If you want to mitigate and reduce risk to your career, your finances, your relationships, and your health before starting your business, read this book.

You will breathe easier.

Most important, you will increase the likelihood that your business will be a raging success.

—Pamela Slim, author, *Escape from Cubicle Nation: From Corporate Prisoner to Thriving Entrepreneur*

Acknowledgments

Writing a book is similar to launching a business. Each requires more time and effort than expected, and most of the sacrifice comes from people other than the author (or founder). Looking back, I'm amazed at how many talented people generously contributed to this project. I cannot name them all here, so I will hit the high notes.

The only thing harder than being married to an entrepreneur is being married to a first-time author. My wife, Kristin, has endured both. She advised and supported me throughout the writing process, providing invaluable feedback on chapter drafts and all kinds of emotional and tactical support. She took on more than her share of responsibility for our family life while continuing to inspire me in her own professional career. Thanks, Kristin, for being my best friend and most trusted editor.

Thanks to Phoebe and Isabelle, for cheering me on while putting up with the strange hours and obsessive habits of a book-writing dad. Phoebe consistently motivated me with her own quiet determination, and Isabelle single-handedly risked life and limb to save thirty pages of a chapter draft that had blown into the street from the roof of my car. Thanks, girls, for encouraging me and for keeping me going.

This book couldn't exist without its central characters. I'm indebted to founders Lynn Ivey (The Ivey), J.C. Faulkner (Decision One Mortgage), Mark Williams (Modality), and Mark Kahn (TRAFFIQ), for their courage, expertise, and openness—and for allowing their founding stories to be shared with the world at large. One of the themes of this book is that launching a business is a highly personal, emotional process. I have not taken it for granted that these founders were willing to be so generous with their lessons learned, and I know readers will benefit greatly from this generosity. I owe a special thanks to J.C., who has been a favorite client, trusted friend, business partner, and mentor for many years now.

Thanks also to other colleagues and experts who lent their voices to the narrative by allowing material from their interviews to be included, especially Chris Holden, Robert (Bob) Tucker, Ken Macher, Shaun Cassidy, John Davenport, Doug Crisp, and Jerry Schiano.

Dawn Ballenger, who came to this book project just as the writing of the manuscript was beginning, has been the person most indispensable to the quality and integrity of the finished product. Dawn spearheaded the book's research, was a close partner in developing the ideas and structure of each chapter, and brought a gifted editorial eye to all drafts. She has also become the rock of Ready Founder Services and ReadyFounder.com, driving our most vital research and product development efforts.

I owe a great debt to David Fugate, founder of LaunchBooks Literary Agency and a thriving entrepreneur himself, who was willing to back a first-time author and provided expert coaching throughout the process. Lori Spangard, of Terrace Blue Marketing, was vital during the project's earliest days, helping me shape first proposals and connecting me with David Fugate (thanks also to entrepreneur extraordinaire Louis Foreman, founder of Enventys and creator of Everyday Edisons, for the assist here).

It's been a pleasure working with the publishing professionals at AMACOM Books, especially Robert Nirkind, who believed in this book and invested more than his share of energy and ideas in making it a reality, and Erika Spelman, who did most of the heavy lifting to bring it past the finish line.

Adam Ortiz, of Executive Development Consulting, has provided tremendous thought partnership and friendship throughout the project. Thanks, Adam, for reading early drafts, for codeveloping the Entrepreneur Core Characteristics Profile (thanks also here to S. Bart Craig of North Carolina State University), and for being a rock-solid business partner.

Thanks also to Mary Bruce, a pro's pro when it comes to business and management consulting, an early believer in the concept of assessing entrepreneurial readiness, and a trusted colleague and business partner.

To Pamela Slim: Thanks for your generosity, leadership, and support for me and for Charlotte's (and the planet's) entrepreneurial community.

In no particular order, for a range of contributions without which this book would not exist, thanks also to: Matt Spangard and the team at Enventys, Daniel Isenberg, Barbara Spradling, Mark Peres, Colleen Gentry, Ted Zoller, Jill Olmstead, Ken Murrah, Bruce Nofsinger, Julie Nance, David Schroeder, Carol Ham, Ben Williams, Suzanne Fetscher, David Dotlich, Peter Cairo, Stephen Rhinesmith, Fletcher Fairey, George McAllister, Ron Meeks, Paul Wetenhall, Phil Hajek, Gary James, Karen Hills, Nancy Owens, Julie Negrin, Richard Goodman, and Jeffrey Kane.

Finally, I am grateful to my parents, Mary and George Bradberry, for instilling in me a curiosity and a love of learning, and to brothers George and Jim and sister Julee. Your teaching and spirit are deeply imprinted throughout this book.

Introduction

"If passion drives you, let reason hold the reins."

—Benjamin Franklin, American statesman
and entrepreneur

You have always dreamed of skydiving, imagining yourself in a free fall, high above the earth, parachute ready to open with the pull of a rip cord.

One day you decide to give it a try. You drive to the local airport and quickly spot the skydiving center at the edge of a wide airfield, far across a parking lot packed with cars. Along the facility's roof are towering letters of blinking red and yellow neon: *Skydive Today. You Can Do It. Do Not Delay!*

You follow a throng of people into the center, where a clerk explains the two options available. The "Basic Option" includes a training program where you will pack your own parachute, with instructor oversight, and learn safety and operational procedures before boarding a plane for your maiden jump. The fee is $250, and there will be a two-hour wait before the training begins. The clerk points to a thin line of customers who are checking cell phones, reading newspapers, and talking quietly among themselves.

But there is also an "Express Option," priced at only $75. For this price, you can grab a pre-packed parachute assembly and hop aboard one of the many express flights without delay. The clerk says that you "should have time" during the plane's ascent to figure out how to operate your equipment before the pilot requires you to make your leap. "You'll have a lot of company," he says, "and you're free to copy what others are doing." He points to a fast-moving line of eager customers, high-fiving each other and congratulating themselves on the thrills ahead.

You hand over $75, grab a pack, and join the crowd in the belly of a massive transport plane just as it begins to taxi toward the airport's central runway. Within minutes, the plane is airborne.

You are on your way.

The above tale may seem far-fetched, especially to anyone familiar with skydiving safety procedures. But the storyline is common in the world of entrepreneurship, where enthusiastic founders often plunge ahead in pursuit of big ideas without adequate awareness or preparation, where unexamined assumptions and unnecessary risks are widespread, and where the personal, financial, and professional stakes of launching a new venture are often exceedingly high. All in a hyped up, do-it-now atmosphere, fed by startup success stories and a support industry eager to sell products and services to aspiring entrepreneurs.

If you are considering your own entrepreneurial leap or have already taken the plunge, you understand the roller coaster of emotions and the powerful pull of freedom and excitement that comes with the commitment to launch a business. For all the challenges faced by new ventures, a lack of passion is not one of them. Entrepreneurs are true believers, famously inspired and optimistic. These qualities are critical, because getting a healthy venture off the ground can be extraordinarily difficult. Successful founders draw from deep wells of conviction and faith to sustain themselves through long days and unexpected challenges.

Entrepreneurial passion is more than an internal emotional state. It is a booming industry, as evidenced by the many books, magazines, websites, products, and services that cater to the natural connection between passion and entrepreneurship, cheering would-be founders to follow their dreams. With enough passion, anything seems possible.

Disenchantment with large employers further fuels startup aspirations. The comic strip *Dilbert* and the hit TV show *The Office* are only two iconic examples of entertainment products poking fun at the absurdity of corporate life. Pamela Slim, author of the best-selling book *Escape from Cubicle Nation*, touched an eon-sized nerve in 2004 when she launched her blog of the same name, aimed at the tens of millions of people desperate to leave corporate jobs to do their own thing. Historically, these disgruntled souls have hung in there because of the relative stability offered by large employers. But this safety net has vaporized over the past two decades as economic upheavals have created wave on wave of layoffs. The once-praised security of corporate America has gone the way of the rotary phone.

Unfortunately, a significant gap exists between this high level of desire and what entrepreneurs actually achieve. Most new businesses fail within a few years of launch. Even investor-backed startups—presumably led by talented founders with better-than-average ideas—fall short at remarkably high rates. And entrepreneurs who survive their first few years aren't necessarily swimming in bliss. The typical new business owner works longer hours, endures greater stress, and earns significantly less over a ten-year period than if he or she had remained in a previous job. Clearly, this is not the world of the fabled *4-Hour Workweek*.

Why This Book?

The purpose of this book is to dramatically improve your odds of entrepreneurial success and enjoyment whether you aim to build a thousand-person venture or a solo consulting practice. It springs from my quest to understand what differentiates successful ventures from the large percentage of startups that disappoint.

In 2007, I set aside my work with large corporate clients to undertake a study of entrepreneurial success factors and work exclusively with early-stage companies, in which I took an ownership stake. I had solid experience to draw upon, having launched a successful consulting business, helped a favorite client turn a blank sheet of paper into a $100 million company, and worked to improve the performance of scores of management teams and a thousand executives over two decades.

As I closely studied the entrepreneurial process, I came to understand that the "secrets" of startup success are not so secret, and not difficult to grasp. The fundamentals that distinguish healthy ventures—principles such as understand your market, know your numbers, get adequate funding, stay flexible, and manage by fact rather than assumption—are well understood by shopkeepers all over the world. But for some reason, many entrepreneurs overlook one or more of these fundamentals, severely undercutting their odds of success.

So I turned to a deeper set of questions: Why do so many entrepreneurs fail to take care of the basics? Why do extremely smart people rush to risk everything on untested business ideas? Why do so many founders underestimate their money needs, adopt pie-in-the-sky sales projections, or miss early signs that things are off track?

Most ventures are driven by passion and belief. Most fail.

Taken together, these statements are hard to reconcile, until we consider the possibility that entrepreneurial passion and startup failure are somehow tightly linked. Could the legendary commitment that drives and energizes so many entrepreneurs be the very thing that leads many of them astray? The more closely I observed the early challenges and choices of would-be business owners, the more clearly I understood how passion plays a powerful and central role in venture success *and* failure.

Drive, determination, fire, belief, optimism, courage, confidence, commitment, certainty, and faith—these are the forces that animate a new business and fuel and sustain entrepreneurs through the ups and downs of the new venture pathway. Each of these qualities, however, when magnified or misdirected, can lead to unhealthy business behaviors—to rose-colored forecasts, to unwise commitments, to inflexibility in the face of new data, or to a catastrophically bad fit between a founder's skill set and the needs of the new business.

It doesn't have to be this way. The good news is that you, as a founder, do not have to choose between passion and reason. You can do what you love and put the full force of your commitment behind your idea, while successfully navigating well-known startup challenges and minimizing inherent risks. This book is designed to help you do just that.

Who Should Read This Book

This book is for:

- *Aspiring entrepreneurs* who are passionate about a business idea and want to dramatically improve their likelihood of success.

- *Existing business owners or founding teams* who want to improve the performance of their venture and their happiness in leading it.

- *Investors* looking for better ways to distinguish winning founders and ventures from the rest of the pack or who want to educate startup teams on the dangers and opportunities associated with entrepreneurial passion.

- *Entrepreneurship educators and service providers* who want a tool to help their students and clients understand the upside and downside of entrepreneurial passion.

- *Anyone* who wants to understand what happens when a person falls in love with an idea and how to best bring the idea to life in a healthy, profitable way.

What Is in This Book and How to Use It

Part I of this book presents and explores its underlying premise: Entrepreneurial passion is a double-edged sword, bringing value as well as danger.

- Chapter One explains what happens within and around a person who commits to the entrepreneurial leap. Why is the startup path so compelling to so many? What causes new founders to become emotionally attached to their ideas, to literally fall in love with their businesses?

- Chapter Two introduces a central concept that every enthusiastic entrepreneur should understand: The *passion trap*, a pattern in which new founders become blinded and constrained by their emotional attachment to a business idea. You will learn the most common negative impacts of the passion trap, and how it sneaks up on unsuspecting founders. I will map the core pattern of the passion trap, a reinforcing loop of ideas, actions, feedback, and interpretation. You will discover how common cognitive biases can sabotage entrepreneurial effectiveness and why some personality types are more susceptible than others. You will also find a list of early warning signs, helping you to flag symptoms of the passion trap when there is still time to counteract its effects.

Part II outlines and explores six principles to help you squeeze the most out of your passion, while not being trapped by it. When applied together, and with the right level of skill, these principles will dramatically improve your odds of new venture success.

1. *Ready yourself as a founder.* The premise of Chapter Three is that the most fundamental driver of your startup's early success or failure is *you.* I will show you how to take an honest look at yourself as a founder; how to align your skills and your role with your venture goals; and how to purify your passion, taking it to a higher, healthier, more productive level.

2. *Attach to the market, not to your idea.* Passion is an inner phe-

nomenon, but all healthy businesses are rooted *outside* the founder, in the marketplace. Chapter Four emphasizes the importance of a *market orientation*, and explains how market-oriented entrepreneurs do three things to ensure that their passion connects with ample opportunity: They obsessively *emphasize* the market; they strive to *know* their markets and core customers; and they *execute* on their market opportunity.

3. *Ensure that your passion adds up.* Most passionate entrepreneurs develop rose-colored plans, over-estimating early sales and underestimating costs. Chapter Five explains the value of developing a clear, compelling *math story*. You will learn how to clearly articulate your business model and plan; how to think about profitability and returns; and how to ensure ample funding so that your venture has room to thrive.

4. *Execute with focused flexibility.* No amount of startup planning can accurately predict the unexpected twists and turns imposed by reality. Chapter Six focuses on the importance of iteration and agility, allowing your venture to be shaped by market forces over time. You will learn the importance of testing and adapting your concept as early as possible, iterating rapidly, and continually improving the fit between your big idea and the marketplace.

5. *Cultivate integrity of communication.* Passionate commitment to an idea can breed reality distortion. Too often, aspiring founders see what they want to see, dismissing uncomfortable facts and avoiding tough conversations. You can avoid these dangers by improving the quality of early-stage conversations and setting a tone for truth-telling and healthy debate throughout your venture. Chapter Seven stresses skills essential for high-integrity communication, outlining four personal attributes that will help you avoid living in a "feel-good bubble": *curiosity, humility, candor,* and *scrutiny.*

6. *Build stamina and staying power.* In an immediate sense, most startups fail because they run out of money or time. Chapter

Eight offers strategies for strengthening and lengthening your new venture runway and for summoning the personal resilience and perseverance that will give your big idea plenty of time to thrive.

In the back of this book, two appendixes provide additional tools and resources to help you launch a successful venture:

- Appendix A features a *Startup Readiness Tool* based on a set of assessment questions I use in my consulting work with new ventures. The questions will help you evaluate your venture's strengths and weaknesses. Are you on solid footing? Where will focused support and attention elevate your odds of success?

- Appendix B includes a resource list of books, websites, blogs, articles, tools, and thought leaders, organized by chapter so that you can delve more deeply into areas where your venture most needs shoring up.

I want to offer one final note on the founders and the storylines that I introduce on the first page of this book. I have included these cases because I know them well—having done advisory work with three of them and getting to know the fourth through an interview process—and also because they illustrate how passion can both elevate a venture's performance and also limit or sabotage success. My intent is to present these stories in a way that is fair, accurate, and unvarnished, so that they represent both successes and failures rather than a romanticized or idealized portrait of the mythical perfect venture. In fact, the further I progressed in the writing of this book, the more clearly I understood that it serves as a sermon to myself, reminding me of my own blunders and my continuing vulnerability to make them again.

In this spirit, I encourage you to harvest the lessons from this book that are most relevant and applicable to your own goals and circumstances. As I think about the teachers and books that have had the greatest positive effect on me, personally and professionally, I can point to lessons from each that have been indispensable, and also, for each, I can point to aspects of their teachings that were not fully applicable or useful to me. I urge you, as a founder, to be a student of yourself and your venture and to use this book as one of many tools in your learning process, creating an approach to entrepreneurship that works for you.

PART I

ENTREPRENEURIAL PASSION

A Double-Edged Sword

CHAPTER ONE

True Believers

Why Founders Fall in Love with Their Ideas

"Following our path is in effect a kind of going off the path, through open country . . . Out there in the silence we must build a hearth, gather the twigs, and strike the flint for the fire ourselves."

—David Whyte, *The Heart Aroused*

The stories of commitment are as different as the founders who tell them:

- Lynn Ivey heard the fear in her father's voice and realized her mother was slipping into the abyss of Alzheimer's disease. "I knew at that moment that my career at Bank of America no longer mattered," she says. "What mattered was my family." That moment led her to leave her bank job as a regional sales executive to care for her mother and, later, to build The Ivey, an adult daycare center devoted to ailing seniors and their caregivers.

- For years, Mark Williams passionately pushed the boundaries of technology, learning, and design. Long before Apple's iPhone revolutionized the use of mobile devices, the Duke University neuroscientist hacked into his medical students' iPods and loaded them with hundreds of anatomy pictures and phrases. The students raved about learning anatomy terms while waiting for coffee, riding the bus, or doing loads of laundry. Mark knew he was on to something, so he launched Modality, a developer of premium learning applications for the iPhone and iPad. "I was so caught up in the beauty of the idea and the possibilities around it," he recalls, "I was not thinking rationally."

- J.C. Faulkner left a senior leadership job at one of America's largest banks to build a different kind of mortgage company and to create a better place to work. "I had come to grips with the fact that all the money I'd saved over a twelve-year career would be gone in six months," he recalls. "When I told the bank that I was leaving to start my own company, I offered to stick around for thirty days to help with the transition. They walked me out the next day—with a box in my hand."

- And then there's Mark Kahn, who tagged along with his boss to a French casino and hit upon a once-in-a-lifetime winning streak. At the $72,000 mark, he turned to his boss and said he was done. "That's smart," his boss said. "You should quit while you're ahead." "No," he replied, "I'm quitting my job. I've got my seed money, and I'm doing my startup." He has since founded two ventures, including TRAFFIQ, a leading online advertising platform listed as number fifty on *Inc.* magazine's 2010 list of America's fastest-growing private companies.

Startups come in all shapes and sizes. Aspiring founders will attempt just about any idea, product, or business model under the sun. If it can be conceived, some dreamer has probably tried it.

Founders take the startup plunge for a dizzying array of reasons: to be free, to change the world, to launch a can't-miss product, to make buckets of money, to follow in Dad's footsteps, or to spend more time with the kids. The list goes on and on, limited only by the fact that a surprising number of entrepreneurs can't fully explain why they do it. They just know that it's something they have to do.

Underneath it all—beneath the endless variation, the unexpected turns, and the wide range of motivations—a powerful force drives everything forward.

It is the force of passion.

When I first began to study entrepreneurship, I would never have predicted I'd be writing a book about entrepreneurial passion. I've always thought of passion as a given in the startup world—a basic ingredient, like salt in food, so common that it would not be a factor in differentiating success from failure. Besides, the topic already gets its share of air time among the great Motivational Media—the hype-driven websites, magazines, books, and videos that have made you-can-do-it success stories into a kind of cult religion for wanna-be entrepreneurs.

But there is no getting around it. Every great venture I've studied has propelled itself forward with an unshakeable sense of commitment, a kind of rapturous belief among core founders. The reason is clear. The startup path is not for the faint of heart. Ask successful entrepreneurs to reflect back on their journey, and an unequivocal response comes back: *I knew it would be hard, but I had no idea it would be this hard.* In the words of technology blogger Dave McClure, "You are going to be embarrassed, ashamed, labeled as an idiot, shunned, ridiculed, and occasionally driven from the village with pitchforks. Get used to it."[1]

On such a demanding journey, qualities that breed confidence and resilience, qualities such as passion, courage, hope, commitment, faith, are like oxygen to entrepreneurs, sustaining them through the long hours, the stress, and the inevitable adversity and doubt that are a natural part of the startup process. But just as oxygen cannot protect a person from all forms of danger, passion cannot eliminate risk from the startup equation. In fact, I have found that passion is just as plentiful among failing entrepreneurs as among those destined to succeed.

As I studied entrepreneurial success factors, I couldn't help but notice the high rates of new business failure, and I became intrigued by the seemingly basic reasons most startups don't make it. The more closely I observed the early choices of would-be business owners, the more clearly I could see the powerful, central role of human emotion. I saw people obsessed with questionable business ideas. I saw founders egged on by friends, family, and motivational speakers. I saw entrepreneurs throwing themselves over the startup cliff without parachutes, sometimes without the merest idea of what they were getting into. I saw impulsive decisions, rigidly held beliefs, wishful thinking, and strategies of hope.

In time, I understood that passion fuels both startup success *and* failure—not exactly an actionable formula you can take to the bank. In the chapters ahead, you will learn how to cut through this apparent contradiction and dramatically elevate your odds of entrepreneurial success. But the first step is to understand what happens within and around a person who approaches the new venture roller coaster. Why is the startup path so compelling to so many? And what causes new entrepreneurs to become emotionally attached to their new creations, to literally fall in love with their ideas?

The Sparks of Entrepreneurial Ambition

Starting a new business uncorks strong emotions that have typically built up over years or decades. Like the winding of an inner coil, an aspiring entrepreneur's early experiences pack potential energy around an embryonic idea and lay the foundation for future startup efforts. Early jobs, both good and bad, further seed entrepreneurial ambitions and ideas. All of this builds toward the day when a founder reaches his or her point of no return, where commitment to the new venture becomes ironclad and all the stored passion and ambition is unleashed.

EARLY FOUNDATIONS

Your preparation for entrepreneurship begins on the day you are born, if not before. Starting a business is an intensely personal endeavor. You bring to it the total package of who you are—your personality, preferences, strengths, and weaknesses. These characteristics are largely developed at an early age, shaping whether or not you will be predisposed to the entrepreneurial leap.

Dan Bricklin, who transformed the computer industry with his invention of VisiCalc, the first electronic spreadsheet, says his entrepreneurial backbone was formed as a kid in Philadelphia, where his father ran a printing business. As a boy, he spent his afternoons helping at the plant and his evenings listening to business chatter around the dinner table. "I suppose you could say the entrepreneurial instinct was in my genes," he says. "My family's unspoken dedication to the business gave me a healthy respect for the paradox of running your own business—the contradictory feelings of freedom and responsibility that define the experience of setting out on your own."[2]

Our early years not only inform whether we will leap at a startup opportunity, but *why* we might do so and what kind of founder we will most likely become. Dan Bricklin credits his religious instruction at a Jewish day school with seeding many of his founding values and skills: his early creative drive; his desire to make the world a better place; and his leadership skills learned by guiding services in synagogue and mentoring other students.

J.C. Faulkner, who built Decision One Mortgage from a blank sheet of paper in 1996 into a company valued at $100 million over four years, says, "I have a memory of when I was in the third grade. When it was time to pick teams, the other kids would look to me and ask 'J.C., who will be the captains today?' They would ask me to settle arguments and make rulings about whether balls were in- or out-of-bounds. I remember one of the teachers asking me how I came to be the one who 'ran' the game, and I said I didn't know. It seemed like it had always been that way." Looking back, he recognizes that he had a knack for figuring out what motivated people, and a strong sense of fairness. Thirty years later, these qualities drove his growing ambition to leave his senior leadership role with First Union Corporation and create a new kind of company, one that attracted and unleashed the best possible talent. His venture, Decision One Mortgage, quickly developed a national reputation as a great place to work with a high performance culture.

For most entrepreneurs, time logged working for others significantly shapes their startup aspirations. In a Fall 2005 article in the *California Management Review,* professor of organizational behavior Pino G. Audia and his graduate student, Christopher I. Rider, noted how early work experience incubates and prepares future founders. "Although some individuals become successful entrepreneurs without related prior experience, they are the exception, not the rule. Entrepreneurs are often organizational products."[3] While working for other people, we develop expertise, serve customers, observe great and awful leaders, and watch untapped opportunities come and go. We appreciate the steady income and soak up the lessons, while our startup ambitions simmer in a semi-conscious stew of hopes and what-ifs.

While studying neuroscience as an undergraduate at Davidson College in the early 1980s, Mark Williams took a summer job to help one of his professors build interactive teaching tools. Their goal was to help students "see" how neural impulses (e.g., auditory or visual signals) traveled through the brain. Using one of the earliest Macintosh computers, Mark worked in a dark basement for months, painstakingly building images. "These were very simple, very crude animations," he says. "We had a 16 color card, and I would zoom these images up and literally move pixels around to create additional colors and make something that looked remotely realistic. I think at the end of the summer we had, maybe, ten seconds of animation that we could control. It was an interesting idea, and we were very passionate about it, but in 1983 we were way ahead of the technology available to us." That summer job was Mark's first taste of how technology could bring together his passions for art, learning, and neuroscience—seeds that eventually gave rise to Modality, his Durham, North Carolina–based mobile learning technology company.

DISSATISFACTION

Whether thinking about retirement, a sabbatical, or a dream business, most working adults fantasize from time to time about the day they will be free to pursue some deeper calling. This yearning, while hard for many to articulate or even admit, can be frighteningly strong, because it springs from a place close to our core. As poet and organizational consultant David Whyte observes, "While we think we are simply driving to work every morning to earn a living, the soul knows it is secretly engaged in a life-or-death struggle for existence."[4]

Most executive coaching clients with whom I've worked over the past two decades are living out their personal versions of this struggle. They are talented, ambitious, and successful—through a corporate lens—but essentially dissatisfied with their professional role. Something else is stirring inside. In working with hundreds of these clients, I've noticed a consistent pattern over the years—the unrelenting pace and compression of their lives, the politicization of their jobs, and the diminishing light in their eyes.

Although he was a fast-rising senior leader within First Union Corporation during the early 1990s, J.C. Faulkner felt increasingly frustrated in his role. "There were some negative things percolating inside of me," he says. "We had an inefficient management team. There was a political sense about us that hurt our ability to compete—too focused on the inside and not focused enough on the competition."

One night, while working late at the office, J.C. helped himself to coffee in the break room. He's not normally a coffee drinker, but needed the boost to get him through a pressing pile of work left by a colleague. He returned the next morning ready to pick up where he left off and was greeted by his boss's executive assistant. She asked if he had been working late, and although he didn't want to admit it, he was kind of glad that somebody noticed.

"What I need to know," she said, "is whether you drank a cup of coffee while you were here. If you did, you owe twenty-five cents for the coffee."

"Well, I drank two cups," he replied. "So I guess I owe you a half a dollar."

The money, of course, was not an issue. What caught him off guard was the bad taste the assistant's response left in his mouth, a familiar feeling of disappointment, disengagement. He was sure that hundreds of employees throughout the division were feeling it as well. "At that moment, I made a promise to myself," he says. "When I create a company, people will never have to pay for spending time at work."

THE EUREKA MOMENT

When he stepped into his evening bath more than 2,200 years ago, Archimedes had grown tired of searching, racking his mind for a foolproof way to measure the true volume of the king's crown (great Greek mathematicians of antiquity were assigned such things). As he absent-mindedly lowered his body and watched the water level rise, something clicked: *Any* object lowered into water will displace an amount equal to its volume. As the story goes, this thoroughly rational man leapt out of his bath and into the streets of ancient Syracuse—naked and ecstatic, shouting, "*Eureka!*" ("I have found it!").

Archimedes's story is an apt metaphor for the emotional journey of most first-time entrepreneurs. Before their *eureka* moments, they puzzle over possibilities, question whether to move forward, wonder how to pull it off, and hope for the right break. They have yet to step into the bath.

Then comes a moment of clarity, a defining event. The future founder is seized by a brilliant startup idea. The puzzle pieces come together with perfect clarity. Things will never look the same again.

Mark Williams recalls the jolt of intensity and excitement he felt as his medical students embraced his first iPod-based learning tools. "A student came up to me and said, 'Dr. Williams, I learned five new brain terms while waiting in line for my latte this morning.'" He said, "And this really represented a *eureka* moment for me. I saw the opportunity to think bigger and more broadly across all types of learning."

To understand Lynn Ivey's *eureka* moment, we must go back to the most transformational month of her life, January 2004. One evening, while having dinner with a fellow manager from Bank of America, she learned that an employee had been missing in action for two days, not showing up at work, not returning calls. The woman was single, like Lynn, and lived in the same neighborhood. Within an hour, Lynn and two others had pushed through the open front door of the woman's home. Minutes later, Lynn found her in her bed, dead of an apparent aneurysm. She was forty-seven years old—Lynn's exact age.

The experience reminded Lynn that life is short and brought her face-to-face with something she hadn't wanted to admit: She wasn't happy with her work. She was far more fatigued than inspired. Within a week, as if on cue, Bank of America announced a plan to lay off 12,000 employees. Two hundred of these were on a national service team Lynn had just spent a year building. The company expected her to shut down the department over the next two months and then transfer into another operational role.

One afternoon, about a week later, her father called. "Your mother has had another episode," he said. "She's really confused, and I don't know what to do." Lynn hurried to her childhood home in Wilmington, North Carolina, on a quest to help her family find comfort and make sense of her mother's deteriorating, unwinding life. Soon she learned that she was eligible for three months of personal leave under the Family Medical Leave Act. She filed for those three months, plus an additional three months of accumulated time off. On her last day with the bank, she cleared out a decade's worth of files and papers from her office, filling a large, two-wheeled, recycling bin to the brim, thinking her banking career was most likely over. "When I walked out, I had my lamp in one hand and a few pictures in the other," she said. "I remember thinking, 'Wow, is this all there is?'"

Over the next year, Lynn sought solutions for her mom's complicated medical needs and her dad's pain. The more she learned about existing services, the more she was convinced of a gap in the market, a need for a comfortable and clean—even luxurious—daycare facility for seniors with memory loss. In addition to her mom's needs, she saw her dad's burden, felt her own, and thought the right care center would bring relief and comfort to family caregivers as well.

Lynn never found the perfect care center for her mom, and as she began to think about what her next career step might be, she inched toward a radical idea. What if she started an adult daycare center herself? Although she knew what the experience should provide—comfort, safety, and stimulation in a warm, nurturing, luxurious environment—she couldn't visualize the component parts. She talked with industry experts and visited site after site, but saw nothing remotely close to her ideal center. Most facilities seemed poorly managed and maintained, lacking even the basics of compassion and comfort.

By the time she visited a center in King's Mountain, North Carolina, she had been searching and puzzling for many months, looking for a model that made sense. She drove up a long driveway to the facility, stunned by what she saw. "It was awesome, on a huge piece of land, with a huge new building," she remembers. "After taking the tour, talking with the director—just seeing the place, the newness and the cleanliness of it—I looked at her and I said, 'This is it. I'm going to do this.'" For the first time, Lynn could visualize *her* facility: how it would look and feel; how staff and guests would move about; and how struggling families would find relief within it. Although she had a number of compelling reasons to pursue her concept, from honoring her mother to addressing what she thought to be a gaping hole in the senior care market, this was the moment when all the pieces first came together into a workable whole.

THE POINT OF NO RETURN

Like Archimedes leaping from his bath, there is a point in every startup journey when hesitancy melts away and there's no turning back. This might take the form of a high profile, catalytic event, such as Mark Kahn telling his boss in a French casino that he was quitting his job or Lynn Ivey buying a piece of land on which to build her future center. But this is not always the case. Sometimes, the corner turned is a psychological one.

Eleven months before J.C. Faulkner left First Union to start his new company, he made a fateful decision while sitting in the office of a trusted mentor, Doug Crisp. Doug, who had hired J.C. into the bank twelve years earlier, was trying to lure him into joining his leadership team in a new bank division. J.C., however, politely turned him down. He said that he appreciated the offer but didn't think a move was right for him at that time. "I haven't accomplished everything I need to do in my current job," he recalls saying.

"Really?" Doug asked. It sounded fishy. He pressed on, asking question after question, refusing to take no for an answer.

But J.C. wouldn't say yes.

Finally, Doug said, "Jay, there's something here I don't know. This is a good promotion for you. Hell of an opportunity. More money than you're making now. And I know you'd love to work for me. What am I missing?"

J.C. paused.

"I'm going to tell you something, and I hope you won't use it against me," he said. "I'm going to leave the bank and start a new company in eleven months. I can't commit to anything new. You need somebody who's going to stick around."

In two minutes, J.C. Faulkner had violated two fundamental rules of corporate success: *Don't turn down promotions*, and *don't share your exit plans with a higher-level leader*. But one of the bank's top executives had flushed him out. "I had a trust level with him," J.C. later remembered. "He's the only guy above me that I would have told about my plans." Looking back, J.C. remembers this as his point of no return, the moment that he knew for sure: He was going to risk everything he'd earned over the past twelve years and leap into an uncertain future as an entrepreneur.[5]

Fanning the Flames of Commitment

Few things in life are as packed with emotion as hurtling down the startup path just beyond the point of no return. Even the most contained entrepreneur feels like he or she has a tiny Archimedes inside, running with happy abandon. There is much to decide and do—hundreds of tasks and questions, large and small. Underneath these practical matters, the founder's growing commitment to the venture is helped along by a set of gathering forces. These forces have been in play all along, like breezes blowing over the first flame of the founder's idea to keep it alive. But now that the point of no return has been reached, they are like winds blowing in from all directions, oxygenating and heating the growing fire.

THE BONDING POWER OF CREATION

Leaders all over the world wrestle with the challenge of getting their team members to care deeply about the goals of a larger organization. They don't understand how employees who are disengaged and apathetic at work can show fanatical passion in their personal lives, organizing citywide fund-raisers on weekends or maintaining Facebook pages with thousands of friends. A core principle is at work here: We authentically commit to those things that we have a direct role in creating. Whether it's a product prototype or a new client account, *I own what I create.*

The same principle applies to your entrepreneurial venture. As you move from idea to action, creating something that can be read, seen, held, tested, or enjoyed in the world, your commitment naturally strengthens. Whether lines of code, a new bank account, a business plan, or a napkin sketch, every new work product puts extra wind in your sails and amplifies your energy and ownership.

Lynn Ivey's dream was becoming more tangible throughout the summer of 2006, and her optimism was contagious. Everyone she encountered came away with a clear, positive picture of The Ivey. They could envision the future building and its staff; they could see a hundred satisfied clients and their relieved families. As a result of her enthusiasm and communication skills, Lynn successfully raised $2.6 million in seed money from investors and secured $3.6 million in loans to finance construction of the center. Groundbreaking was scheduled for October. In late July, she sent an e-mail to several of her supporters, writing, "The money's raised and in the bank!! The loan's approved and closing is at 9:30 a.m. this Tuesday!!"

About that same time, Lynn's father called and asked her if she would make the four-hour drive home to Wilmington. "He's putting Mom on oxygen," she wrote at the time. "He says she is really winding down and thinks she'll be getting worse soon. It's ironic... my mother is the whole reason I started down this path to create the center. If she shuts down now, it will be as if she knows that phase one of my creation is complete and that it really will happen. I'm a believer that when God shuts a door, he always opens a window."

BELIEFS MADE REAL

Why do we commit to certain business ideas and not others? How do our beliefs become so rock solid that they are virtually impossible to dislodge? Most businesspeople think of commitment as an intangible force. They know it when they feel it, but don't see any underlying mechanisms to explain how something so "soft" actually works. But research into how the brain works sheds considerable light on the fact that such mechanisms not only exist at a neurological level, they exert great power as well.

In a 2007 study, neurologist Sam Harris and two collaborators investigated the role of various brain regions and structures in mediating our beliefs. They measured how long it took people to judge written statements as "true," "false," or "undecidable," and they scanned their subjects' brains during the process using functional magnetic resonance imaging (fMRI). They found that people assessed statements as believable more quickly than they judged statements to be false or undecidable, and that the different types of statements were processed in distinct regions of the brain. In short, new information that matches our existing perceptions gets an "express lane" treatment, whereas contradictory information takes a longer, more tortuous processing path. "Because the brain appears to process false or uncertain statements in regions linked to pain and disgust," the researchers wrote, "this research supports [the seventeenth century philosopher] Spinoza's conjecture that most people have a low tolerance for ambiguity and that belief comes quickly and naturally, whereas skepticism is slow and unnatural."[6]

Researchers have also found that deep levels of passion create significant changes in the brain, changes that, in turn, reinforce the very beliefs that created them. Andrew Newberg, M.D., director of the Center for Spirituality and the Mind at the University of Pennsylvania, has studied the brain's role in spirituality and written extensively about the topic. He and his collaborators have scanned the brains of hundreds of religious practitioners (Franciscan nuns engaged in prayer, meditating Buddhists, Pentecostal followers speaking in tongues), documenting how beliefs become neurologically real in the minds of practitioners. He even scanned the brain of an avowed athe-ist, who was asked to attempt to pray to God, and concluded that when a person is asked to adopt beliefs contrary to his own, the brain often applies the brakes, so to speak. "If the pieces don't fit well together, a neurological dissonance is created that sends an alarm to other processes in the brain."[7]

With each passing day, Lynn Ivey found more reasons to believe. In November 2006, a month after her mother passed away from com-plications related to her dementia, she received an e-mail from a woman who had read about The Ivey in a local magazine. "You do not know how much I have prayed for someone like you," the woman wrote, going on to share that her husband was declining due to a re-cent, massive stroke, and she was entering her own battle with breast cancer. "Please tell me that you will be open soon and that there is some availability. Could you send me some information? Lynn, you are a GOD SEND! I had always thought a higher-class daycare would be a great thing to do. If you need any help at all, I would love to help out, but first I need you to OPEN!"

YOUR FEEL-GOOD GANG

The entrepreneur's path can be crushingly lonely. New founders must find and haul their own motivational fuel, building their store of inner resources. At the same time, nearly all successful entrepre-neurs find support and encouragement from their social network of friends, family, colleagues, and advisers. One of our earliest instincts during the incubation phase is to share our idea with trusted friends and colleagues, people who can act as sounding boards and who might caution us about unseen obstacles or problems. Mostly, we hope they will reinforce our idea, confirm the rightness of our path, and cheer us onward.

On this last hope, the news is all good. Studies investigating the impact of social networks on the formation of new ventures suggest that when a founder seeks support and advice for a new venture, he or she taps a small number of well-known, trusted, and like-minded individuals.[8] And social psychological research has confirmed again and again that we are an unfailingly polite species when asked for any kind of evaluative feedback. In one intriguing study conducted by psychologists Bella DePaulo and Kathy Bell in 1996, test subjects were put in the difficult situation of critiquing an artist's paintings for which they had already privately expressed a dislike. They had never met the artist or known of the artist's work. Nearly everyone was hesitant to say anything that might discourage the artist or give rise to hurt feelings; the most blatant white lies coming from people who had been told that the artist cared deeply about a particular painting.[9]

The upshot of this and other studies is that the more openly we share our passion for our new venture, the more likely it is that we will receive support and encouragement, not only from the usual suspects—trusted friends and family—but from just about anyone who can see our enthusiasm for the business idea. Lynn Ivey talked with hundreds of people within and outside the senior care industry as she formulated plans for The Ivey, and she found nearly universal support for her concept for an upscale daycare center located in the Charlotte, North Carolina, area. With a few exceptions (to be explored in later chapters), "Your center will fill up in no time," was the common refrain, she heard from industry professionals, investors, and old friends alike.

THE WIDE WORLD OF MOTIVATION

It's Saturday morning. You've decided to finally do something about that gnawing feeling of settling for someone else's dreams. Today is the day you seize control. Coffee in hand, you flip open your laptop and Google the word *entrepreneurship*. The first featured link at the top of the page catches your eye. It reads "Easily Started Businesses." You click on it and see, in forty-point font:

RENEGADE PHYSICIST DISCOVERS 57 SECRET IDEAS THAT COULD MAKE YOU RICH!

Welcome to the Motivational Media. If you haven't fully convinced yourself that your business idea has potential, or if you doubt you can pull it off, just turn on the TV, open an entrepreneurial magazine, or surf the Web. You'll find a thousand smiling entrepreneurs, posing in front of swimming pools and Maseratis, eager to tell you how they did it and bring you into their startup fold. You will be amazed at how happy and proud they are, and how *many* there are. You can watch the Y.E.S. movie (by the Young Entrepreneur Society), starring white-toothed motivational speakers. You can surf entrepreneurial comment boards, where fellow dreamers decry "negative and unsupportive people." You can peruse a *Start Your Own Business* magazine with a hundred get-rich-quick schemes. And you can read a recent book encouraging the younger generation to go ahead and make the entrepreneurial leap, offering advice like, "Don't worry if you don't know what you're doing. Nobody does!"

Plenty of worthy information does exist for aspiring entrepreneurs, if you can cut through all the noise and clutter (I have included a listing of my favorite sources in Appendix B at the end of the book). It seems, however, that the following themes dominate most of the startup content floating around these days: (1) Starting a business of your own is the surest way to happiness and wealth, (2) Everybody's doing it, or will, (3) Ignore nay-sayers who don't support your dream, and (4) The only thing holding you back is . . . *you!*

There is one more theme. Most of these sources of encouragement have a strong commercial interest in your taking the entrepreneurial plunge. Their mantra: "You can do it—we can help!" My favorite example comes from a 2007 promotional campaign from Intuit, maker of small business accounting software. Its stated purpose was to move aspiring entrepreneurs from saying, "I wish I had just started my own business…" to saying, "I just started my own business!" It was called the "Just Start" campaign and hosted at www.IWillJustStart.com. The campaign was Intuit's response to survey data, collected from a paid vendor, suggesting that four out of five working adults in the United States dream of starting their own business some day (with no mention, of course, of the high percentage of startups that fail). It's not clear how many aspiring business owners "just started" a business as a result of the campaign or how many software products were sold as a result, but the campaign surely stoked the startup fires among thousands of founders in waiting.

AND NOW, A WORD FROM THE UNIVERSE

Students of religion, philosophy, or self-help will note that the motivational atmosphere around entrepreneurship has a familiar ring. It mostly parallels historical traditions that encourage self-discovery and self-improvement. Celebrated U.S. mythologist and writer Joseph Campbell reminded us that the powerful theme "Follow Your Bliss" resonates through ancient stories and myths of all cultures.[10] Likewise, adherents of The Law of Attraction, a positive thinking concept popularized in 2007 in the movie and book *The Secret*—and one that proliferated quickly through the you-can-do-it blogosphere—dates back to the world's earliest societies.

One of the most well-known passages ever written on the topic of commitment was attributed to the nineteenth-century German writer Goethe, who wrote "Whatever you can do or dream, you can do, begin it. Boldness has genius, power, and magic in it. Begin it now."[11] I was influenced by this passage during the 1990s, as I prepared to quit my salaried position (as a husband and a father of a six-month-old girl) to start an independent consulting practice. And I've shared similar materials with my clients from time to time, bringing relevant historical wisdom to the challenges of today.

The point here is that optimism travels well, and it has done so across the ages. It's as if some god of startups has been active all along, century after century, provoking fervent belief and bold action among merchants, traders, dreamers, and adventurers of all stripes. If you are looking to find encouragement and further stoke your passion for your new venture, material is readily available from all directions, all centuries, day or night.

If You Build It, Will They Come?

Lynn Ivey's unshakeable commitment to her cause has come down to this. Three and a half years after she has left her bank job, she and I are sitting in the high-ceilinged main room of The Ivey, her sparkling $4.5 million adult daycare facility. Although it is midday, we are nearly alone in the center. Only a couple of staff members are around to care for the two clients who have signed up so far.

We're taking a break from another tough meeting about The Ivey's dire financial situation. Lynn, two key investors, her attorney, her accountant, and I have worked through the morning, playing out various revenue and expense scenarios. Although the fire has not left Lynn's eyes, it's been a morning of grimaces and long faces. With virtually no sales after nine months of marketing to prospective members, she is in danger of running out of money within six months. Her expense base is weighty, due to the high-end nature of the facility, her passionate attention to every detail, and the fact that she must keep a minimum professional staff on board to meet regulatory requirements.

We talk about what has been learned over the past year. Lynn had projected a sold-out center at this point in time and had invested significant resources into promoting the facility—direct and indirect marketing campaigns, including reaching out to referral sources like geriatricians, in-home care services, assisted-living facilities, and the like. While the pipeline of interested prospects has buzzed with activity, the number of families scheduling tours has amounted to a trickle.

"Oh my god. I almost forgot," she says with a self-deprecating laugh. "You won't believe what I did this weekend. My nurse, Betsy, rented my favorite movie of all time, *Field of Dreams*, and I must have watched it three or four times. I had forgotten some of the scenes, and I couldn't believe how perfect it is for what I'm doing here." I ask her what scenes were most on target.

"Remember James Earl Jones at the edge of the baseball field, his speech to Ray when the bank's about to foreclose on his house? It's perfect." She peels back a few pages on a worn white legal pad and begins to read aloud from James Earl Jones's famous speech, only this time he's talking about The Ivey. He's describing how customers will come for reasons they can't understand; how they will drive from miles around and knock on the front door; how they will hand over their money, innocent as children, in search of peace and comfort, and hungry for the past.

As I listen, I feel a gut-wrenching mix of admiration for Lynn's resilient faith and deep concern for the facts on the ground. I'm thinking about all that is at stake here, quite a few jobs and lots of money, but mostly Lynn Ivey's dream of taking care of families in need and her attempt to honor the mother who had taken such great care of her.

If there *is* a god of startups, how can this venture fail?

CHAPTER TWO

The Passion Trap

How Attachment to Your Idea Can Sabotage Your Startup

"If you want a recipe for a startup that's going to die, here it is: a couple of founders who have some great idea they know everyone is going to love, and that's what they're going to build, no matter what."

—Paul Graham, founder, Y Combinator

According to Greek mythology, a boy named Icarus and his father, Daedalus, were held as prisoners on the island of Crete with no possible route of escape by land or by sea. But Daedalus, a skilled craftsman and inventor, had developed a plan to escape through the air. He secretly built wings for himself and Icarus, using reeds and feathers held together by wax. As Daedalus attached the wings to his son's arms, he warned him to fly at the right altitude. If he flew too low, the salt spray from ocean waves would soak his wings; if he flew too high, the heat of the sun would cause them to melt.

After escaping the island by flying out over the sea, Icarus was exhilarated by his newfound freedom. Despite his father's warning cries, he flew higher and higher, circling closer to the hot sun where the melting wax and feathers began to separate from his arms. The wings disintegrated, and Icarus plunged to his death in the water that now bears his name, the Icarian Sea.

The tale of Icarus parallels a story I have watched unfold again and again among passionate entrepreneurs. You take a risky leap. You experience the elation of newfound freedom. You boldly fly higher with single-minded conviction, ignoring nay-sayers who shout warnings from below. Then you find yourself in some irreversible crisis with no way to overcome gravity's downward pull.

The culprit in this story is something I call the *passion trap*, an all-too-real phenomenon that undermines many a new venture. The passion trap has roots in a basic truth: Your intense devotion to your business concept can bring danger along with its obvious benefits. Passion provides courage, energy, and optimism to propel you on your flight forward, but it also can blind and deafen you to helpful data and ideas. And it can lead you to believe that you're somehow immune to typical startup risks that wise founders have learned to respect and manage.

Anyone who cares deeply about his or her startup idea is subject to being snared by the passion trap. It is an equal opportunity affliction, governed by a set of well-known emotional patterns and biases that come with being human. Seasoned entrepreneurs and successful investors alike can recognize the damage done by unchecked or misdirected passion.

The good news is that you can have it both ways. You can bring high-flying enthusiasm and confidence to your startup and also protect yourself from being blinded—or blindsided—by your emotional attachment to an idea. Of the many forces that might derail your startup dreams, the passion trap is one that is squarely under your control. With awareness and the right practices, you can be certain that your entrepreneurial zeal will work for you rather than against you.

The purpose of this chapter is to explain why and how entrepreneurs get caught in the passion trap and what happens when they do.

I'll survey the damage done—in the form of six negative impacts of entrepreneurial passion—and examine the personality characteristics that predispose a person to getting caught in the trap. I'll also share a list of early warning signs to help you assess your own vulnerability. Then, in the second part of this book, I'll outline and explain six principles that will significantly elevate your odds of converting your big idea into a healthy, thriving business.

What Is the Passion Trap?

The passion trap is a self-reinforcing spiral of beliefs, choices, and actions that lead to critical miscalculations and missteps, mistakes such as significantly underestimating what is required to get a business off the ground; greatly over-assuming initial customer interest; making deep, irretrievable commitments to unproven concepts; and, in too many cases, rigidly adhering to a failing strategy until it's too late to recover.

One of the most dangerous aspects of the passion trap is the subtle, illusory way it takes hold. On the surface, it masquerades as the kind of heroic determination that fuels every startup success story. Passionate business owners show boldness, commitment, and clarity of purpose—qualities we all crave, qualities that *feel* good. Whether or not you identify with the confident swagger of Virgin Group's Richard Branson or Apple's Steve Jobs, it's hard to deny that they seem to enjoy what they do.

However, when an entrepreneur becomes too emotionally attached to an idea, boldness can be transformed into arrogance. Commitment narrows into a kind of tunnel vision. Cognitive biases filter and bend incoming data to conform to the founder's hopes and beliefs. Conversations are drained of objectivity. Even worse, these patterns are generally invisible to the founder, and their negative impact is usually delayed over time. Like a termite-infested home, the seemingly solid startup is eaten from within.

The Damage Done: Six Negative Impacts of Entrepreneurial Passion

Why should an aspiring entrepreneur be concerned about passion? What kind of startup problems are caused by misdirected enthusiasm? Among a range of impacts, the most common negative consequences fall into six major categories.

FOUNDER MISALIGNMENT

New entrepreneurs often struggle to find the best fit between what they personally bring to the table (strengths, weaknesses, needs, and hopes) and what the new business requires. The more passionate the founder, the more likely he or she will drift toward one of two extremes. At one end are founders who focus only on what they love to do, thereby neglecting other important areas of the business. In this scenario, the entrepreneur's passion becomes an end in itself, rather than something that fuels a higher business purpose. He or she confuses positive emotion with progress, and "feeling good" becomes the moment-by-moment measure of success. At the other extreme are founders who try to do it all, taking on roles that don't play to their strengths, spreading themselves too thin and refusing to let others take up the slack. In this case, new business owners become overextended and overwhelmed while the startup challenge grows in complexity, urgency, and scope.

I remember a conversation with Mark Williams in early 2006, not long after he raised his initial funding for his idea to create learning products for the Apple iPod. "I'm going way too fast," he told me, "and I'm going nowhere at all." Mark was working at breakneck speed with a couple of software developers to design and build Modality's first product prototypes. The work was obsessive but clunky—one step forward, two steps back. He was frequently traveling to New York and Philadelphia to wrestle with publishers over licensing deals and to California to meet with key Apple representatives. His remaining time, like scarce butter on toast, was spread thinly across everything else in the business—forecasting a budget, planning an office move, designing a brand, and assembling the pieces of an e-commerce por-tal—all of this while being continually jerked around by the unex-pected daily crises that define startup life. "At that time, you're doing everything," he remembers. "You're not sleeping, of course. You're working around the clock. You're incredibly intense about meeting deadlines that are externally imposed. You're running this race against all kinds of unknowns."

Mark had reached a breakpoint that required him to expand his team and let go of key task areas. We talked about the importance of the founder's role in building longer-term capacity and discussed how he could position himself over time to exploit his strengths and cover for his weaknesses. Looking back, he remembers how challenging it was to "make a pit stop," as he called it, to bring on additional talent and offload some of the work. "There was such a great dialogue be-tween the two or three people I was working with at the time," he re-calls. "It was very natural and nonverbal—unconscious in many ways. We had been together from day one, so bringing additional people into the fold was a struggle for many, many reasons." But by doing this difficult work, Mark and his team began to generate much more MGP (his acronym for "making good progress") on all essential fronts.

A related problem with founder alignment is seen in freedom-crazed entrepreneurs, who dive headlong into startup adventures with little awareness of how their founding role in the new venture will ad-versely impact their loved ones and their well-grooved lifestyle. At the startup's inception, they envision a thriving venture and happy families all around. Then the realities of getting a business off the ground begin to sink in—the never completed to-do list, the mind constantly riveted to work-related challenges, and the fact that fami-lies and friends usually sacrifice more than expected. If expectations and reality are not aligned, new founders can be overwhelmed with unnecessary stress, fatigue, and guilt.

MISSING THE MARKET

Most startups suffer from anemic early sales, far below projections. In too many cases, the uncomfortable truth is that expected market demand for a new product or service, demand that is critical to the startup's viability, simply doesn't exist. A classic misjudgment on the part of the founding team is usually to blame: *We believe passionately in this product, so everyone else will, too.* It's a build-it-and-they-will-come mentality, where the entrepreneur knows better than the customers what will make them happy. Too often, this attitude gives rise to in-spired products that never find more than a few customers, or bril-liantly conceived solutions in search of problems to solve. Even when a robust market opportunity does exist, over-confident founding teams rarely invest enough time, energy, and resources into marketing and selling their offering. They assume that the world will beat a path to their doorway. And they routinely underestimate, or dismiss alto-gether, the strength of competitive forces that will impact success.

Based on votes of confidence from her many friends and col-leagues, as well as encouraging market data and her own deep sense of personal mission, Lynn Ivey planned to start signing up future clients in May 2007, four months before The Ivey's scheduled grand opening. She decided to target wealthy families, who would pay out-of-pocket for an exclusive, club-like atmosphere, positioning The Ivey as an exception to other drab and depressing senior facilities. Her clients would be known as "members" and would pay an upfront membership fee of $3,000, as well as a weekly fee for attendance.

The Ivey's business plan forecast sixty pre-registrations from May to September, which would generate $180,000 in registration fees. Ac-cording to plan, one hundred members would sign up by the end of 2007, resulting in over $1 million in client revenues for the year (a fig-ure thought conservative by Lynn and her team, as it didn't include revenue from planned ancillary services, such as transportation, spa services, gourmet meals-to-go for caregivers, etc.).

To accomplish the sales task, Lynn hired a full-time marketing professional in January 2007 and engaged the services of a local mar-keting firm. She presented the sales plan to her experienced, well-connected board, and the group generated additional marketing ideas. Everyone seemed to know families who would be perfect prospects for The Ivey's services, and board members were eager to help open doors with prospective corporate and institutional partners.

By the end of June, after two months of active sales efforts, Lynn and her staff were confused as to why no members had enrolled but remained confident that there was still plenty of time to generate sales momentum before the fall. Throughout the summer, Lynn received regular inquiries from curious families, but she saw few prospects that were both qualified and willing to move forward. After a barren summer led to still no sales through September, her puzzlement turned to concern.

Ever the optimist, Lynn had a two-pronged explanation. First, discussions with prospective client families were proving to be more complex and lengthy than originally thought. Spouses and children of declining seniors were grappling with emotional family issues of denial and guilt, and major care decisions often involved multiple children living in different parts of the country. Second, even though The Ivey had invested in colorful wall-sized renderings of the facility and world-class marketing materials, Lynn became convinced that having a finished building to show prospective customers would be the key to generating expected sales. A series of delays had pushed the center's grand opening out until November, and she eagerly anticipated this event as the magical point when prospective members and their families could see the grandeur and comfort of the facility for themselves. No more abstract descriptions of the service—just oohs and ahs from touring families hungry to sign up.

But the lack of sales, combined with facility delays, were straining The Ivey's financial picture. During the third week in October 2007, Lynn communicated to her board the need for approval to raise more investor capital. "The Ivey has a need for additional funding," she wrote. "The primary reason is that I missed the boat completely when projecting that we would have sold many memberships from a virtual sales office prior to construction completion." In closing, she wrote "I'm really sorry that I'm having to request this at this time. However, I am confident that we will fill up as soon as prospective members begin to see the facility."

Not long afterward, Lynn and her staff moved into the new building, a dazzling 11,000-square-foot-resort-style lodge. The cedar shake and stone facility features a huge great room with wide windows, a massive stone fireplace, and vaulted ceilings, along with many other specialized rooms for activities and programming, a "tranquility room," a physical fitness room, a craft and movie room, a full-service kitchen, and a library.

Although families began signing up for on-site tours, sales remained alarmingly low. By the end of 2007, only a few members were on board, generating revenues of less than $10,000 for the year, approximately 1 percent of projected sales. Head scratching and sleepless nights continued. Worse yet, at a time when her every minute should have been focused on solving the mystery of The Ivey's missing market, Lynn was faced with the gargantuan task of coming up with another $1.5 million.

ROSE-COLORED PLANNING (OR NONE AT ALL)

Passion-trapped entrepreneurs are unrealistically optimistic. Secure in their belief that they've discovered a can't-miss idea, they view the startup journey through rose-colored glasses. Best-case assumptions drive plans and projections. Projected revenues and expenses are based on what's possible, rather than on what is practical or likely. As a result, founders caught in the passion trap are blissfully unaware of how long it will take, in realistic terms, to reach their financial breakeven point and what it will cost to get there.

As entrepreneur/investor Guy Kawasaki notes in his book *The Art of the Start*, aspiring entrepreneurs often fall into the trap of "top down" forecasting when sizing up a business idea.[1] The founder starts with a large number, representing a population or a market to be targeted, then works downward from that number to generate expected revenues for a new product. As an example, let's say you've developed a new technology for restaurant owners, priced at $10,000 per unit. There are about 215,000 full-service restaurants in the United States, and you believe that you will be able to capture 1 percent of this market over three years. This would result in 2,150 product sales or $21.5 million in top-line revenue over a three-year period. Sounds good. And even if you forecast only one-fifth of that number for year one, 430 units, you're on track for more than $4 million in sales in your first year.

But startup plans must be executed from the bottom up, where the math works differently. Suppose you can afford to begin with a team of three sales professionals, working full time, who can each sift through two hundred leads a month to generate twenty onsite demonstrations. Let's assume these twenty demonstrations will land each salesperson an average of two sales per month, equaling 1 percent of monthly leads (if you think that's a pessimistic number, you've never tried to get a restaurant owner to part with $10,000). This sales rate would generate twenty-four sales for the year for each salesperson, or seventy-two sales for the team as a whole. That's $720,000 in first-year revenue, with a lot of assumptions baked in about having skilled, active salespeople on board, supported by marketing, technology, and infrastructure, all of which will require significant upfront costs and ongoing management and servicing expenses. Based on these bottom-up assumptions, you would need a team of thirty salespeople working over three years to achieve your goal of capturing a 1 percent market share. This is not outside of the realm of possibility, with the right product, the right plan, the right funding, the right talent, and the right breaks, but cracking one percent of any market generally requires a herculean effort. Simply forecasting downward from a large available market won't make it so.

Although passion can lead to over-optimistic planning, a surprising number of fast-moving founders avoid planning altogether. They plunge forward and manage by feel, without an accurate read on where the business stands. They tend to operate in a financial fog, and, lacking the focus of a clear game plan, they can be pulled and distracted by an endless stream of new money-making ideas. As someone who hears a lot of new business pitches, I'm struck by how often ambitious entrepreneurs visualize global expansion or exotic product extensions long before they have won their first paying customer. As management researchers Keith Hmieleski and Robert Baron noted in the June 2009 *Academy of Management Journal*, highly optimistic entrepreneurs often see opportunities everywhere they look, a distracting tendency that can interfere with their ability to effectively grow their new ventures.[2]

This challenge applies to seasoned businesspeople as well as first-timers. In fact, Hmieleski and Baron have shown that experienced entrepreneurs are actually *more likely* to suffer from overconfidence and "opportunity overload" than those with no startup experience.[3] Entrepreneur Jay Goltz may be a case in point. He writes a highly insightful column for *The New York Times*'s Small Business Blog, has launched many ventures over the past two decades, and employs more than one hundred people in five successful businesses. "Did I mention that four of my businesses failed?" he writes. "In my case, it wasn't market conditions or competition or lack of capital . . . It was my penchant for jumping into things with blind optimism and not enough thought. I'm a recovering entrepreneuraholic. I'm trying to stop."[4]

AN UNFORGIVING STRATEGY

There has never been, nor will there ever be, a shortage of new business ideas or aspiring founders willing to commit time, sweat, and tears to bring them to life. Unfortunately, many of these ideas, perhaps the vast majority, don't represent achievable business opportunities. Jeff Cornwall, director of the Center for Entrepreneurship at Belmont University, estimates that 40 percent of startup failures are simply due to businesses that should never have been launched in the first place.[5] John Osher, successful, serial entrepreneur and creator of hundreds of consumer products, goes even further. He has developed a well-circulated list of classic mistakes that he and other entrepreneurs have made, and first on his list is what he considers the most important mistake of all. "Nine of ten people fail because their original concept is not viable," he says. "They want to be in business so much that they often don't do the work they need to do ahead of time, so everything they do (going forward) is doomed."[6]

Because early ideas are so frequently off the mark, surviving and thriving as an entrepreneur means treating the startup journey as an exercise in uncertainty. The future is unknowable. No matter how thoroughly you research your target market, or how rigorously you plan your startup launch, your first strategy will most likely be wrong. So, too, will your second. In the few weeks, months, or years it takes to launch your product or service, the world will change. New obstacles and opportunities will appear as you accelerate along your learning curve. Unpredictable events will occur, some good, some bad, and highly anticipated outcomes may never materialize. For this reason, startup success requires that you allow for quick, early failures as you put your ideas into action. This means building plenty of flexibility into your business model so that you can integrate relevant lessons and adapt to new conditions.

Unfortunately, passionate and overconfident founders sometimes put the lion's share of their available resources into a singular, high-cost strategy, leaving no cushion or wiggle room for things to go wrong, or to go differently, as they inevitably will. This bet-the-farm approach can require major outlays of capital before key assumptions can be tested in the real world. All the eggs are in a single basket, and few good options remain when the basket hits the ground.

When bulldozers first began clearing and grading The Ivey's future site, Lynn Ivey believed that her prime location and the high quality of her planned facility, surrounded by thousands of wealthy, aging households, would prove to be the cornerstone of her dream. The building was carefully designed and custom built from the ground up. Every brick, curtain, color, and piece of furniture conformed to the greater ideal. But constructing the facility and getting a full staff in place required a $4.5 million capital commitment that would, over time, weigh Lynn down like an anchor around her neck. In addition to building and maintenance costs, zoning and regulatory factors constrained her ability to use the building for other commercial purposes, with the notable exception of hosting weekend events like wedding receptions and retreats.

It seems Lynn was caught in a classic unforgiving strategy: Large upfront capital requirements had used up most of her "dry powder" and incurred a heavy debt burden, all before her basic concept could be tested. She lacked a viable contingency plan for revenue shortfalls, which proved to be severe, and, other than approaching friends and family for private loans, she found few options when her money began to run out. She considered opening The Ivey to all older adults, creating a kind of "well seniors club," but worried that the concept wouldn't mix well with her mission of serving cognitively challenged older adults. The lack of members eventually forced her to bring her prices down by nearly 70 percent, to a level equal to other adult daycare centers (many of them nonprofits with dramatically less overhead). This increased the number of members slightly, but put The Ivey further into a financial hole. She would need to find a consistent, high-level revenue stream if The Ivey was to survive.

New businesses that call for heavy investment in facilities or infrastructure before the first offering of a product or service incur much greater risk than most other startups. Lynn Ivey did consider, very early in her planning process, the idea of leasing temporary space in order to test her concept with a lower expense base, but she determined that available spaces wouldn't allow for her envisioned atmosphere of luxury and comfort.

THE REALITY DISTORTION FIELD

Andy Hertzfeld, a member of the first Macintosh computer software development team in the early 1980s, credits fellow team member Bud Tribble with coining the phrase "reality distortion field" to describe the driving, charismatic influence that Apple co-founder Steve Jobs, carried over the team. "The reality distortion field was a confounding mélange of (Jobs's) charismatic rhetorical style, an indomitable will, and an eagerness to bend any fact to fit the purpose at hand," he writes. Once they understood Jobs's ability to bend reality, team members puzzled over how to respond to it. "We would often discuss potential techniques for grounding it," Hertzfeld writes, "but after a while, most of us gave up, accepting it as a force of nature."[7]

Steve Jobs is certainly a force of nature, and his confident, forceful style has driven Apple Computer to great heights over the years. The same quality drove him to leave Apple in order to launch NeXT Computer in 1985. Jobs believed that his NeXT cube system, aimed mostly at high-end academics, would change the world of computing. Jobs secured a high-profile investment partner in Texas billionaire

Ross Perot, who later called the investment "one of the worst mistakes I ever made," then sprinted forward in pursuit of his big idea. After building a state-of-the-art manufacturing facility ready to crank out 150,000 units a year, NeXT sold only 50,000 computers over the life of the company. The product was critically acclaimed, even coveted, in technology circles, but it was much more expensive than competing systems and so advanced that the typical user found limited practical value. "He believed that the company couldn't fail," wrote technology columnist, Colin Barker, in October 2000. "In the end, the story of the NeXT cube became a study in failure. NeXT was a high-profile disaster, a computer system that the world admired but wouldn't buy."[8]

The NeXT example provides a cautionary tale for all entrepreneurs because every founding team creates its own reality distortion field somewhere along the startup path. "Drinking the Kool-Aid" is a very common early-phase business activity. After building overly rosy plans, founders are swayed by psychological pressure to seek out data that validate their vision and to avoid or deny bad news. Unspoken group norms promote disdain, even hostility, toward people who raise concerns or point out contradictory data. These pressures combine to create a kind of psychological cocoon around the startup team and its founding premise. The business is assumed to be on a destiny-driven path.

Steve Jobs is only one of many successful entrepreneurs who have found that world-class intellect and leadership skills won't protect them from the occasional dangers of reality distortion. J.C. Faulkner, the most talented entrepreneur I have ever worked with, temporarily lost touch with his own solid instincts when he attempted, two years after his tremendously successful launch of Decision One Mortgage (D1), to start a new telemarketing subsidiary in April of 1998. Despite concerns on the part of his original D1 leadership team, J.C. lured an intact management team from another company to set up and run the new business, to be called Home Free Mortgage, and hired sixty call center employees to occupy an entire floor of office space. He decided to oversee the new initiative himself, thinking that he wanted to keep his D1 leadership fully focused on growing the core business. But members of his D1 team grew increasingly worried about cracks in the Home Free model and the lack of experience in its management team. Uncharacteristically, J.C. brushed off these concerns.

When mortgage markets took a nosedive a few months later, J.C. and his original team spent most of a day debating Home Free's deteriorating financial situation. The conversation was skillful and brutally honest—so much so that the reality and gravity of the situation became abundantly clear. J.C. decided to shut down Home Free the next morning. It was an excruciating decision; he had worked tirelessly for more than six months to recruit the Home Free team and negotiate a deal to extract them from their previous company (a fact that prompted some dark humor from his banker, who told him that "he dated the company longer than he was married to it").

Although J.C. had arranged for his original team members to have ownership stakes in Home Free, he decided to absorb the entire loss himself. Looking back, he jokes that he personally earned $8 million that year from D1 and *lost* $8 million on Home Free. But more painful than the financial loss was the experience of telling employees that he was closing the company after only four months, and then shortly thereafter meeting with his local D1 staff to explain his mistake.

The launch and demise of Home Free Mortgage serves as a kind of photographic negative for all that went right about the D1 launch. D1 is the positive case study and Home Free is the anti-case, occurring because a talented entrepreneur got swept up in passionate pursuit of a pet project that never would have withstood his usual level of scrutiny and analysis. "In a sense, I was in a hurry to prove that D1 wasn't luck," J.C. now says. "I had some ego confusion, so I was very quick to try to prove that I was smart. What I did—very quickly and very expensively—was prove just the opposite." I once asked him what he would he have done differently, had his judgment not been fogged by overconfidence. "I would have dug into their financials," he says. "I would have spent more time. I would set up a real clear structure, start out with a small amount of money, get profitable on a small scale, and then replicate it. I would have done the things I did when I started D1."

AN EVAPORATING RUNWAY

Until the new business concept has proven itself and is generating a sustainable level of revenue, startup founders must deal with a pile of ever dwindling resources. The first five negative impacts all increase the likelihood that a new entrepreneur will run out of cash, time, support, or personal will before he or she can find an adequate revenue stream. Exerting additional pressure on desperate founders is a rule I find myself repeating to every aspiring entrepreneur who shares startup plans with me: *Everything will take longer and cost more money than you think.* This principle underscores the importance of developing realistic, hype-free estimates regarding your new venture's pathway to profitability, so that you can set realistic timelines, secure adequate resources, and identify behaviors and practices that will maximize your startup's staying power.

The Core Pattern: How the Passion Trap Works

It's clear that the above negative consequences can drag down otherwise talented founding teams and significantly reduce a startup's probability of success. But, specifically, how does entrepreneurial passion play a role in these outcomes? How can positive emotions, so vital in propelling a great idea forward, also undercut a startup's odds of success?

The answer lies in a simple, sneaky pattern, a looping interaction between internal factors (such as a founder's biases, perceptions, and choices) and forces that operate outside the founder (such as actions, data, and results). The pattern feeds and strengthens existing beliefs and biases—what we think is true, and what we *hope* to be true—about the startup idea we are putting into action.

THE FOUR INTERDEPENDENT STEPS OF THE CORE PATTERN

The core passion-trap pattern consists of four interdependent steps, each leading to the next (as shown in Figure 2-1):

1. *Attachment to an Idea.* Whether through an incremental process or a single bolt of inspiration, you latch onto a compelling business concept: a cool product, an innovative service, or an unstoppable mission. It's good. You know it. And you can feel your enthusiasm building. The more you think about it, the more excited you get. Your emotional attachment grows, and leads to . . .

2. *Investments and Actions.* You invest time, energy, money, or other resources and move forward with your idea. This can include many different actions, depending on how far you have gotten along your startup path—sharing your idea with colleagues, exploring the Web, talking to potential customers, hiring team members, or building a prototype. These actions give rise to . . .

3. *Feedback or Results.* Early actions always lead to something that can be seen, heard, and evaluated—the reactions of friends and family, information about customers and competitors, a duct-tape version of your first product, or even early sales results. These results are then subject to . . .

4. *Biased Interpretation.* At the heart of the passion trap is the enthusiastic entrepreneur's well-documented tendency to notice and embrace information that supports existing beliefs and to discount or completely miss contradictory evidence.

Figure 2-1. The core pattern of the passion trap.

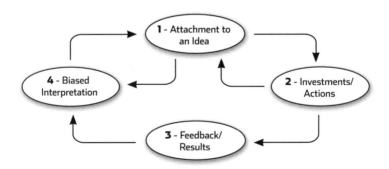

This selective filtering process is governed by a set of subtle but powerful cognitive biases operating just beneath the founder's awareness. As a result, he or she develops an even stronger emotional attachment to the idea, and the cycle rolls forward. Wash. Rinse. Repeat.

Not only does each step in the pattern lead to the next in a self-reinforcing cycle, but smaller reinforcing loops are at work as well. As discussed in Chapter One, when you invest in an idea and start to make it real (oval 2 in Figure 2-1), you strengthen your attachment and commitment to it. And, as your attachment to the idea grows, so does the likelihood that your biases will distort incoming reality (oval 4 in Figure 2-1).

THE ROLE OF COGNITIVE BIASES

If there's a single psychological concept that every aspiring entrepreneur should understand, it's the phenomenon of cognitive biases. Cognitive biases are mental and emotional filters that help us make sense of the constant barrage of information coming at us every minute of every day. They determine how we frame our interactions with the world, where we focus our attention, what patterns we select, what data we see as important versus irrelevant, and how we reach conclusions. Like software programs running quietly in the background of our mental computer, these biases operate continually and reflexively. As with blinking and swallowing, they are always at work but rarely noticed.

For the most part, cognitive biases are tremendously helpful, allowing us to make quick judgments and navigate through an increasingly information-rich world. It would be impossible to get through our day without them. But they also play a central role in perpetuating the passion trap, leading to errors in reasoning and the recycling of flawed assumptions and choices. In one sense, launching a business is nothing more than a rapid series of decisions, one after the other, and startup founders must continually improve their ability to recognize patterns, analyze these patterns efficiently, then make the right calls, all at a rapid-fire pace. In growing D1 from a blank sheet of paper into a successful national competitor, J.C. Faulkner didn't think of his business as being about mortgages. Instead, he focused on making quick, high-quality decisions and on building a team and a culture that could do the same. "That's the core business we were in," he says. "Making great decisions efficiently."

In the startup environment, the importance of making good decisions is complicated by the naturally high levels of passion and emotion associated with launching a big idea. As we saw in Chapter One, the mechanisms that reinforce our beliefs operate at a neurological level, where thoughts and emotions are tightly intertwined. No choice is made at a purely intellectual level. In fact, a good deal of research in cognitive psychology and neuroscience suggests that emotions drive our decision making processes, even when we are completely unaware of their role.[9]

Of the many biases that sabotage our startup reasoning, here are a few that every startup founder should understand, as they are especially likely to trip up entrepreneurs who are passionate about their idea:

- *Confirmation Bias*—our tendency to select and interpret available information in a way that confirms our pre-existing hopes and beliefs. Lynn Ivey, for example, heard a lot of positive feedback about her idea for a high-end adult daycare center, but she can also recall some notable dissenters: a former healthcare system CEO, who thought in-home care services would be a formidable competitive force; a board member, who was concerned that customers wouldn't pay such high fees; and an expert on services for the aging, who felt a for-profit center would never work. These views were easily dismissed and drowned out by supporters, whose opinions paralleled her own. In retrospect, the dissenting views form a pattern of concern. But at the time, they were just isolated exceptions to a clear majority.

- *Representativeness (belief in the law of small numbers)*—the tendency for entrepreneurs to reach conclusions based on a small number of observations or a few pieces of data. Entrepreneurship researchers have concluded that startup founders often fall victim to this bias, because they operate in uncertain and fast-moving environments where facts can be hard to obtain.[10] The new founder who hears positive reviews from three out of four friends and then assumes that 75 percent of the general population will react similarly is under the spell of representativeness. It's also in play when a wanna-be entrepreneur reads a magazine's worth of success stories and assumes much higher success rates than actually exist across the general population.

- *Overconfidence/Illusion of Control*—these are actually distinct cognitive biases, and each has both positive and negative impacts on entrepreneurial success.[11] Overconfidence leads founders to treat their assumptions as facts and see less uncertainty and risk than actually exists. Illusion of control causes business owners to overrate their abilities and skills in controlling future events and outcomes. Both of these tendencies drive entrepreneurs to develop rose-colored plans and fail to prepare for inevitable bumps in the road. One study of startup ventures across a range of industries, for instance, found that more than 80 percent failed to meet confidently established market share targets.[12]

- *Anchoring*—our mind's tendency to give excessive weight to the first information we receive about a topic or the first idea we think of. This bias is all about the stickiness of first ideas and impressions. It encourages founders to cling to an original idea or, if pressed, to consider only slight deviations from the idea instead of more radical alternatives. An example of anchoring is the role it plays after initial sales or cost targets are set by a founding team. Even if the forecasts are wildly optimistic (as they often are), they continue to serve as anchors for future planning processes, influencing forecasts toward unrealistic levels.

- *Escalation of Commitment ("sunk cost" fallacy)*—the tendency to continue or increase commitment to an endeavor based on prior investment of money, time, and energy. Startup founders may refuse to abandon a losing strategy in an attempt to preserve whatever value has been created up to that point. Paul Graham, accomplished entrepreneur (Viaweb) and investor (Y Combinator), refers to this phenomenon as the "still life effect," based on his experience as a painter. He noticed his tendency to continue painting a poorly arranged composition (a bunch of stuff "plonked" on a table) simply because of the time already invested in the project. This parallels a common approach among startup teams. "You come up with a random idea, plunge into it, and then at each point (a day, a week, a month) feel you've put so much time into it that this must be *the* idea . . . Plunging into an idea is a good thing. The solution is at the other end: to realize that having invested time in something doesn't make it good."[13]

Icarus Qualities: Who Is Most Vulnerable to the Passion Trap?

The story of Icarus flying too high for his own good serves as a stark reminder that certain human qualities can become liabilities if taken to extremes. Optimism, for example, is a typical entrepreneurial trait that improves performance, *but only up to a point.* In fact, moderately optimistic people have been shown to outperform extreme optimists on a wide range of tasks and assignments.[14] This is true for a number entrepreneurial characteristics, qualities that can be amplified to unhealthy levels by unrestrained passion. I call them "Icarus qualities" because they are vital to startup flight and must be present at some level (remember, Icarus was warned about flying too low as well as too high), but when overdone, these qualities can cause founders to fly too close to the sun:

- *Confidence/Optimism.* Successful entrepreneurs tend to believe in a brighter future. They are not easily deterred by others' negativism or criticism. However, at extreme levels, confidence begins to function as arrogance or blind certainty. The role of overconfidence in startup failure has been well-documented, leading Mathew Hayward and two collaborators to formulate a "hubris theory of entrepreneurship," asserting that the high-risk world of startups attracts people who are overconfident by nature, and that this overconfidence, in turn, plays a key role in perpetuating high venture failure rates.[15]

- *Need for Achievement.* Call it drive, ambition, or competitiveness. Successful entrepreneurs desire to fly higher and higher and are unshakably committed to their cause. At extreme levels, this high level of drive can show up as a volatile, my-way-or-the-highway approach that alienates partners and customers alike.

- *Independence.* Successful entrepreneurs are often willing, or even inclined, to strike out on their own. They can shoulder the pangs of loneliness that all startup founders experience. But extremely independent business owners can become stubborn and aloof, sealing themselves off from access to constructive feedback, resources, and other sources of help and support.

- *Creativity/Imagination.* Many entrepreneurs are classic dreamers, full of ideas and aspirations. They see potential where others see nothing. They ingeniously create awe-inspiring products. Unfortunately, extremely imaginative founders can fall in love with ideas that other people don't "get" or need. They lose touch with what matters most to others—to customers, team members, investors, etc.

- *Risk-Taking.* Effective startup founders are skilled at evaluating and assuming calculated risk. At its extreme, a propensity for risk-taking drives entrepreneurs to take risks for the sheer excitement involved (much like gambling) or, in concert with too much optimism, to believe that their risk-taking is aligned with some greater destiny.

- *Follow-Through/Focus.* This is a critical capability for early-stage businesses, where resources are usually scarce and distractions abound. But a passion-trapped founder with single-minded focus can get stuck in a narrow tactical rut, stubbornly sticking to an outmoded game plan, while the startup ship takes on more and more water.

In Chapter Three, I will outline a full set of entrepreneurial characteristics that are conducive to startup success. At this point, I encourage you to compare yourself against the above list and identify where your personality may be vulnerable to overheated enthusiasm. As you do so, consider this: Was Icarus a born risk-taker, wired to be impulsive and overconfident? Or was he swept up by remarkable events that might lead any person to want to cavort with the gods? After all, it's not every day that a guy escapes from a lengthy captivity *and* finds himself flying like a bird. Put differently, was Icarus driven by an enduring trait or caught up in a temporary state?

These same questions apply to your own personality and your role as an entrepreneur. Even if you possess only moderate levels of a trait, you might experience, during the first heady days of a startup launch, temporary shifts in emotion or behavior that *look and feel very much like an extreme form of that trait.* If you suspect that you are "not yourself" during the adrenaline-crazed rush of the startup phase, you may be right. Whether trait- or state-driven, the above tendencies taken to extremes will increase your odds of being trapped by your startup passion.

Early Warning Signs: Are You in Danger of Being Trapped?

It's hard to differentiate between healthy optimism and blind optimism. Below is a list of early warning signs to help you evaluate whether you are in danger of undercutting your odds of startup success. The more accurately the following sentences describe you or your startup, the more likely you are exposing your new business to unnecessary risk. Are you . . .

- Thinking or saying, "This is a sure thing?"
- Losing patience with people who point out risks or shortcomings in your plan?
- Believing your solution is better than anything on the market?
- Feeling full of energy but lacking focus and traction?
- Measuring progress by how good you feel?
- Expecting most of your sales to come from word-of-mouth or "viral" marketing?
- Assuming that you are entering a space with little or no competition?
- Counting on immediate revenue to avoid financial problems?
- Plotting global domination before releasing your first product?
- Lacking clarity about where your business stands financially?
- Delaying product releases until they are perfect?
- Preventing things from happening without your involvement and approval?
- Loving your product, with no idea who will buy it?
- Hearing great "buzz" but finding few (or no) paying customers?
- Finding yourself saying (about your customers), "They don't get it yet, but they will!"?
- Thinking that planning is a waste of time?

Moving Forward: Six Principles for Making the Most of Entrepreneurial Passion

As you continue on your startup journey, the core patterns and cognitive biases described in this chapter will continue to play a role. You cannot completely erase them, nor would you want to. They will help you cut through the noise and clutter of the startup process, and your passion for your business will bring the energy necessary to accelerate your startup forward. But if you agree that passion poses dangers as well as benefits, you can apply a set of six principles to squeeze the most out of your startup enthusiasm while not being trapped by it. These principles also correspond to, and offer solutions for, the six areas of negative impact discussed earlier in this chapter:

Area of Negative Impact	Corresponding Principle
Founder Misalignment	*Founder Readiness.* Chapter Three will show you how to take an honest look at yourself and what you bring to the table as a founder; how to align your skills and your role to achieve your startup goals; and how to purify your passion, taking it to a higher, healthier, more productive level by *understanding* it, *connecting* it, *strengthening* it, and *directing* it.
Missing the Market	*Attach to the customer, not your idea.* This principle addresses the primary paradox facing entrepreneurs: Passion is an inner phenomenon, but all healthy businesses are rooted *outside* the founder, in the marketplace. Chapter Four will explain what a *market orientation* is and how it will bring your venture an edge over product-centric startups.
Rose-Colored Planning	*Ensure your passion adds up.* Chapter Five will illustrate how your business can be reduced to a simple, clear, and compelling *math story*. You will learn the power of clearly articulating your business model and plan, how to think about

profitability and returns, and a few principles for funding your venture so that your passion has room to thrive.

Unforgiving Strategy

Agility. No amount of planning can accurately predict the unexpected twists and turns imposed by reality. Chapter Six will focus on the importance of finding ways to test and adapt your concept as early as possible, iterating rapidly and continually improving the fit between your big idea and the marketplace.

Reality Distortion Field

Integrity of Communication. Agility enables success only if your decisions and discussions are grounded in reality. Integrity of communication places a premium on the quality of early-stage conversations and sets a tone for truth-telling and healthy debate. Chapter Seven will focus on how to cultivate high-integrity communication and will outline four personal attributes that help founders burst the "feel-good" bubble: curiosity, humility, candor, and scrutiny.

The Evaporating Runway

Staying Power. In an immediate sense, most startups fail because they run out of money or time. Chapter Eight will outline two sets of approaches for extending and strengthening your available runway: (1) *venture-level strategies*, such as launching close to the customer, addressing big risks early, raising more money than you think you will need, and committing resources wisely, and (2) *founder-level strategies*, such as feeding your fire, focusing on achievable goals, balancing performance with recovery, and persevering without attaching.

PART II

YOUR FOUNDATION

Six Principles for Launching a
Can't-Miss Startup

CHAPTER THREE

Founder Readiness

How to Prepare for the Entrepreneurial Journey

"It's not the will to win, but the will to prepare to win, that makes the difference."

—Paul "Bear" Bryant, legendary college football coach

As Scott Shane notes in his book, *The Illusions of Entrepreneurship*, most new businesses fail. "Pretty much all studies agree on that," he writes. "The only question is how long it takes for a majority of them to go out of business (and why)." Startup failure rates are consistent across different types of companies, across different parts of the world, and across decades. Even investor-backed startups, presumably led by talented founders with better-than-average ideas, fall short at remarkably high rates. "In short, no matter how you measure new firms and no matter which developed country you look at," says Shane, "it appears that only half of new firms started remain in business for five years, and less than one-third last ten years."[1]

More troubling—and telling—is the state of entrepreneurship among ventures that *survive*. Only one-third of all owner-operated businesses in the United States generate $10,000 or more in annual profits. The typical business owner will make 35 percent less over a ten-year period than if he or she worked for someone else during the same period. And, contrary to conventional wisdom, this lack of financial success is not offset by greater job satisfaction. On average, people who own their own businesses work significantly longer hours and experience higher levels of stress, fatigue, and depression than people who work for someone else.[2] Based on these facts, startup founders are clearly not achieving happiness or creating wealth at a level consistent with all the hype and hope surrounding entrepreneurship.

A primary reason for the dismal statistics concerning startups is that too many passionate founders confuse their optimism with *readiness*. At the moment of their entrepreneurial leap—the very point at which the personal and professional stakes could not be higher, the time when knowledge and preparation will make all the difference—emotions escalate and passion takes over. Driven by impatience and unwavering belief, aspiring entrepreneurs plunge forward without adequate awareness of what their new business will require and how well they match up against those requirements.

The solution lies not in ratcheting down passion, but in elevating awareness. By pausing early in your startup process to take an objective look at yourself and what you bring to the table—your purpose, goals, skills, resources, and needs—you can develop a highly valuable kind of optimism, one that rests on the rock of clear, honest assessment and willful preparation. I call it *earned optimism*, and I find it to be much more useful than the uninformed hope that drives many startup founders. It is a quality worth pursuing. Earned optimism will boost your performance and help you sleep at night.

As a reference point, most of us can recall an opportunity from our past that we approached with confidence and passion, but with little awareness about what the opportunity called for, whether it was a marriage that ultimately ended in divorce, a job that didn't work out, or a business project that went sour. With the benefit of hindsight, it's instructive to look back and consider how we would have approached the opportunity differently, and more skillfully, had we only known then what we know now.

Years from now, after your startup journey is complete, what questions or issues will you wish you had thought about in advance? What will you regret having learned the hard way? As a new founder, while the clay of your idea is still moist, you have the opportunity to stand on the shoulders of hundreds of millions of entrepreneurs who have come before you, to leverage the wide body of existing knowledge about what works and what doesn't. The premise of this chapter is that the most fundamental driver of your startup's early success, or failure, is *you*—your purpose, goals, skills, personality, relationships, resources, and needs. These factors will either enhance or diminish your ability to achieve your startup dreams and, just as important, determine your level of happiness as you pursue them.

The Fundamentals of Founder Readiness

It's hard to imagine a founder better prepared to launch his or her chosen startup than J.C. Faulkner. On the personal side, J.C.'s capacity for empathy, his natural charisma and self-awareness, and his initiative, communication, and interpersonal skills were all evident long before he launched D1. Professionally, he spent twelve years learning the fundamentals of mortgage lending, navigating the up-and-down cycles common to the industry. He led a number of First Union's sales branches and regions across the United States, turning many of them around from under-performing to high-performing units. In the process, he got to know a lot of talented, well-connected people in a highly relationship-driven industry. And he gained a decade's worth of leadership experience, building sales and service teams and managing bottom line results of large, high-growth business units.

Despite his expertise and experience, J.C. took the time to patiently prepare himself and his startup plan until the window of opportunity was right. "It took me a year and a half," he says, "from waking up one day and thinking I could be doing this, to getting up one morning and saying I *should* be doing this." He studied the marketplace, developed an initial game plan, recruited a colleague to build financial models, and quietly began lining up prospective investors. "I was ready, emotionally, long before I could piece it together logically.

I wanted to be prepared mentally, so I spent that time learning as much as I could at my current job."

Similarly, long before Mark Kahn's three-day winning streak in the French casino, he prepared himself for his entrepreneurial leap. Over eight years, he rotated through a series of increasingly challenging digital media jobs in Rupert Murdoch's News Corporation, a global media juggernaut built in the image of its entrepreneurial founder. "It was really a great proving ground to be part of that," he recalls, "with this spirit of entrepreneurship living in every operating unit. Even though there were hundreds of operating units, each one sort of lived on its own and acted as though it was a startup company." During those eight years, he gained experience in a broad range of disciplines, including technology, marketing, corporate finance, and general management. When Mark left the company in 1998 to build a family of e-commerce sites on the early Web, his former boss, a rising News Corp. executive named Chris Holden—the one who had stood beside him in the casino, shocked and bemused, as he won an unexpected $72,000 in startup cash—watched his venture with interest. He knew Mark Kahn would bring a rare blend of intelligence, drive, and skill to his startup challenge.

Few aspiring entrepreneurs bring the high level of relevant experience and preparation of a J.C. Faulkner or a Mark Kahn. In fact, most founders plunge forward with more haste than preparation, injecting unnecessary risk and challenge in to their startup path. These cases underscore a set of truths that stand out to me after years of participating in and studying new venture creation:

- *Founder readiness makes a difference.* A founder's (or founding team's) level of fitness and preparation directly and significantly impacts startup success or failure.

- *No founder is a perfect fit for his or her chosen startup.* Therefore, every founder can improve on level of readiness and odds of success.

- *Founder readiness is an ongoing challenge.* All entrepreneurs can and should continually evaluate and improve their fitness to lead their company forward.

Founder readiness is the principle of bringing your absolute best to your entrepreneurial effort, finding the best fit between your goals and capabilities and the needs of your new venture. This means understanding what you bring to the business, as well as anticipating what impact the business will have on you and the people you care about. Although it's true that founders shape startups, it's also true that startups shape founders. Your entrepreneurial role will test your character and expose your strengths, weaknesses, desires, and fears. Clarifying these issues at the start heightens your competitive advantage and allows you to have your cake and eat it too: You can bring rabid enthusiasm to your venture, doing what you do best and what you love to do, while also having the confidence that you've considered and addressed the areas of greatest challenge and risk. From an investor standpoint, the principle of founder readiness acknowledges the critical nature of the talent in whom you are investing. How well does the founder's motivation and expertise match up with the needs of the proposed venture?

You can improve your readiness to succeed as a startup founder by undertaking five basic steps:

1. *Clarify your reasons and your goals.* Why are you doing this? What do you hope to achieve?

2. *Understand your entrepreneurial personality.* Who are you? What makes you tick?

3. *Map your skills and experience.* What can you do? What do you know?

4. *Leverage your relationships and resources.* Who can help you? What assets are available for your use?

5. *Position yourself for high performance.* Are you optimally positioned to bring your "A" game—your best effort, energy, and performance?

In this section, The Fundamentals of Founder Readiness, I'll further explore each of these five areas. The framework mirrors a readiness assessment process that I conduct with new clients to help them strengthen their venture foundation. These questions will help you better understand your passion and your skills and how these relate to your chosen venture. In the final section of this chapter, Purifying Your Entrepreneurial Passion, I'll revisit the principle of understanding passion and provide three additional principles for making the most of your passion: *connect it, strengthen it, and direct it.*

CLARIFY YOUR REASONS AND YOUR GOALS

Whenever I meet someone who wants to start a business, the first question on my mind is: *Why? Why are you doing this? Why now? What are your reasons, and what outcomes are you hoping to achieve?* The answers to these questions will drive both the direction of the venture and how effective the founder will be in getting it off the ground.

All reasons are not created equal. Each comes with benefits and tradeoffs. What follows are nine common reasons for plunging down the startup path, along with a few important considerations for each.

INDEPENDENCE/SELF-RELIANCE - If the freedom to call your own shots appeals to you—if you want to set your own priorities, work at your own pace, and be your own boss—you are in league with most aspiring business owners. The more autonomy-driven you are, the more you might prefer to operate as a sole proprietor or freelancer, rather than as part of a founding team.

"Being your own boss" is more myth than reality for most entrepreneurs. Every successful business owner must consistently answer to others: customers, creditors, suppliers, and investors. Understand how your independent streak might constrain your bottom line and limit your growth prospects. Research confirms that businesses started by two or more co-founders succeed at higher rates than those run by sole proprietors.[3] And if you are interested in growing the value of your business over time, you will, most likely, need to complement your strengths with those of others and relinquish some control of your business to funders or other business partners.

ACHIEVEMENT - If you are motivated by challenge, driven to be the best in a particular field, want to prove to yourself that "you can do it," see a better way of doing something, want to do work of highest quality, want to stretch, learn, and get better—all these are positive signs for the future of your new business. The drive to achieve is one of the most potent and lasting motivators because it comes from within, can be focused on the concrete steps vital to advancing a startup, and isn't easily weakened by challenge or adversity.

The early days of a startup can be frustrating for achievement-driven founders because many important tasks and activities don't lead directly to measurable outcomes. Given that paying customers may not be a reality for some time, the more clearly you can define what constitutes meaningful progress, the more your drive to show progress can be directed in fruitful and satisfying directions. In Chapter Five, I'll share ideas for clarifying goals and priorities early in your startup process.

FINANCIAL GAIN/WEALTH - You may view starting a business as the best way to earn a good living or as the road to wealth creation. This latter ambition is often a special case of the drive to achieve, where money functions as a way of keeping score and a means to other ends. Even after financially driven entrepreneurs have earned more money than they and their families will ever need, they continue to be lured by the great game of commerce and the thrill of the deal. In the eyes of venture investors, this drive toward financial success is usually a positive sign. As Chris Holden of Court Square Ventures notes, "Those who are most motivated by a return on their personal sweat equity and the risks that they took, the money that they raised, and their own money that they put in it, those are the ones who are most willing to adapt to changing conditions, and be transparent, and to not care about being liked or how they look. . . . They don't let anything get in the way of their real goal, which is to succeed." Chris's experience is supported by a Kauffman Foundation study published in June 2009, examining the personalities and motivations of 549 successful startup founders across a range of industries. Seventy-five percent of these founders "expressed a desire to build wealth as an important motivation in becoming an entrepreneur."[4]

Bringing realistic financial expectations to your startup journey

will be vital to your success. The road to startup wealth usually requires financial sacrifice in the early going, sometimes extended over
many years. Well-prepared founders are willing and able to operate
at reduced income levels as long as necessary. If financial motivation
is the *only* thing driving you, you may not be willing or able to handle
the economic realities of early-stage startup life.

HIGHER CALLING/MISSION – Some entrepreneurs are passionately
driven by a special cause or a higher calling. Their animating fire
cannot be quenched. Lynn Ivey personifies this reason for starting a
business. I've met very few people who bring her combination of un-
shakable belief, optimism, and energy to their startup effort. As we
will see in later chapters, Lynn's personal sense of mission propelled
The Ivey through some very tough sledding. This is true across the
startup landscape in the form of many mission-driven founders, who
seem to draw energy and inspiration from a source greater than
themselves.

Unfortunately, mission-driven founders may be more likely than
others to become trapped by their passion. Their confident certainty
and sense of destiny can blind them to the more sobering aspects of
building a business, and they may be slow to understand that their
mission and message won't resonate with everyone. If you feel driven
by a higher calling, be sure to surround yourself with reality checks
to counterbalance the stubbornness that can come with inspiration.

MARKET OPPORTUNITY – Of all the reasons to start a business, I believe most strongly in this one as a predictor of ultimate success.
When founders are driven to address a known gap in the marketplace,
their energy is directed precisely where it should be—on solving an
emerging or existing customer need. They are much more likely to
build their new business on a foundation of solid market demand. J.C.
Faulkner has always been an entrepreneur in waiting—it's stamped
in his DNA—and so it was only a matter of time before he made his
startup leap. But his specific idea for D1 sprang from his timely
recognition of an emerging gap in the marketplace. He was passionate
about catching the coming wave of home finance activity and designed his venture to do so.

If you are obsessively driven to solve a customer problem, be sure to do your homework by testing your assumptions about the size and readiness of your chosen market. It's not enough to successfully solve a problem. You must solve a problem that customers will pay to have solved in sufficient numbers and at a price that will generate a healthy return for your business over time.

AN ESCAPE FROM SOMETHING – Many, many people want to pursue self-employment because they are desperate to break free from a dead-end job or a bad boss. They may feel bored or stagnant or fear that working for others no longer provides the security it once did. Or, they may have been laid off and cannot find any reasonable options in the current job market.

Although it's understandable that such situations provoke many of us to finally take the startup plunge, these kinds of "away-from" reasons, unless they are accompanied by an even stronger "toward" motivation, do not typically drive entrepreneurial excellence. The further a new founder moves from a distasteful situation, the less motivational power these reasons pack. Starting a business is hard; people don't succeed simply because they were unhappy or unsuccessful at something else. If you are driven by dissatisfaction with your career or life situation, try to identify and cultivate more forward-looking motivations, reasons that would cause you to abandon a *great* situation because they are so emotionally or intellectually compelling.

LIFESTYLE – Some founders are primarily motivated to run a business that meshes with their desired lifestyle *outside* of work, but achieving your dream lifestyle while building a healthy business may be more difficult than the hyped-up entrepreneurial media would have you believe. It's true that technological innovations have led to an explosion of home-based, Web-based free agents across the world (bloggers, Web designers, Twitter consultants, SEO marketing specialists, etc.) and you can now outsource almost any task that you find daunting or uninteresting. But most of these free agents don't earn enough to cover basic living expenses,[5] and those who do make a good living at it will readily admit that they work around the clock to lift their product or service above the abundant noise and clutter of the Web.

In the case of Tim Ferris, author of the best-selling book *The 4-Hour Workweek* and father of a worldwide movement of "lifestyle design,"[6] it's clear that he has put in herculean hours and effort in promoting his book, building his brand, and marketing his image across the world. In mastering any profession or a craft, the appearance of a radical shortcut is usually illusory. If it seems too good to be true, it usually is. Achieving your ideal lifestyle will likely require tough choices and sacrifices.

SOCIAL/COMMUNITY – Some founders are driven to entrepreneurship because they want to work with friends, be part of a great team, meet new and interesting people, or create a vibrant community of co-workers, customers, or colleagues. J.C. Faulkner launched D1, in part, because he wanted to create a better place to work. "My motivation was more personal than professional," he said. "I wanted to build a place where I could attract talented people and treat them better than they'd ever been treated and where I felt better about working. I would have taken a cut in pay to do this. In fact, I thought I *was* taking a cut in pay."

The instinct to start a business with friends or family is as old as commerce itself, and it's common for founders to end up on startup teams because friends recruited them into the role. I worked for many years with a successful and superbly led global consulting firm that grew out of the collegial friendships among its three founders. For the most part, they saw working with each other and having fun together as the primary reason for joining together in a business. In this case, the founders' social motivations served the venture well, contributing to trust-based relationships and alliances inside and outside of the business.

The inherent risk associated with starting a business with friends has been well chronicled. Just because you like a person or went to school with that person doesn't mean he or she is a good fit for the business you are launching. I've enjoyed healthy business partnerships with close friends, but, in every case, the business relationship made sense and worked well independently of social factors.

***INNOVATION/CREATIVITY/ARTISTRY* –** Many aspiring entrepreneurs are driven to pursue a technical innovation or a unique product idea, to turn a specialized hobby or craft into a job, or to build something that has value apart from themselves. I group these motivations together, because the common animating force is the age-old thrill of making something from nothing. Founders driven in this way see their new ventures as crucibles in which this creation can occur. It's a powerful motivator, and a close cousin of the need to achieve. Mark Williams, founder of Modality, is a great example of a founder who is obsessively, passionately, unreasonably driven to create the perfect product. Such founders are typically creatures of the lab, the studio, or the computing platform. Any opportunity that allows them to pursue their creative passion is one they will gladly embrace.

The challenge for founders driven by innovation and creativity is finding markets that are both sizable and ready for their craft. Researchers, "creatives," software hackers, and product developers are often leery of marketing and sales activity and lack general business acumen. If your first love is innovation, learn to respect market and financial forces and the talented people who understand them. They will help you tether your passion to sustainable streams of good fortune.

There are, of course, other reasons to start a business. Some people feel that they were born to be entrepreneurs and will jump at the first opportunity. Others want to go deep into a professional specialty or follow in a family tradition of entrepreneurship. Whatever your reasons, work to understand what is driving you and how this might impact your startup approach.

Alongside the question of why you want to start a business is the question of what you hope to accomplish. Even if sketched out in very general terms, articulating your goals puts a stake in the ground and helps you to further think through your overall level of readiness. I use the following questions with clients as a starting point:

- *Briefly describe your business concept in 50 words or less: What will you offer? For whom? Why is your concept unique or compelling?*

- *What do you hope to achieve—personally and professionally—over the short-term (next 1–2 years)? What about the longer-term (5+ years)?*

There are no perfect answers. Start by brainstorming a list. Write down whatever comes to mind and then narrow the list to those items that are challenging and compelling enough to drive energy and effort, directional enough to guide week-to-week choices and behaviors, and clear and simple enough to keep front of mind.

Here are some examples of early founding goals I've heard:

- Spend no more than $30,000 over the first year of operation and generate positive monthly cash flow after nine months.

- Become known as the go-to expert in specialized healthcare training for the greater Nashville region within two years of launch.

- Launch an initial website within three months and have accurate per-customer metrics in place within four months.

- Build a company that is valued at $10 million or more within seven years.

- Develop my team to the level that allows me to take two consecutive months off each summer to spend with family, within three years.

As you can see, goals can vary considerably in terms of time horizon and focus (personal or professional). Only you can determine what success looks like as you move forward. The more concrete your starting goals the better, although they shouldn't be etched in stone. They will need to evolve as you learn more about your market opportunity (Chapter Four) and clarify your business model and "math story" (Chapter Five).

UNDERSTAND YOUR ENTREPRENEURIAL PERSONALITY

I have found that the founder's unique set of personal characteristics, more specifically, the degree of *fit* between the founder's personality and the needs of the new venture as it evolves, has a far-reaching impact on whether or not his or her goals are achieved. The key is to understand what personal characteristics are most likely to drive success for your new venture, honestly assess your own personality relative to these characteristics, and decide how to address any significant gaps.

Successful entrepreneurs tend to be:[7]

- *Commercially Oriented.* They are interested in money and business and are driven to achieve bottom-line profitability. They focus on tapping new revenue opportunities and instilling their startup with financial discipline and cost-containment.

- *Conceptual.* They are idea people, continually unearthing new opportunities. They are "emergent learners," adaptively learning from experience and experimentation. They are intelligent, are able to skillfully deal with ambiguity and complexity, and have the ability to discern useful patterns from large amounts of information.

- *Independent.* They are willing or inclined to strike out on their own. The isolation of entrepreneurship is sometimes inescapable, and every founder must, at times, stand apart from the herd.

- *Achievement Oriented.* They are passionate, ambitious, competitive, and driven. They love a challenge, enjoy mastering new skills, display a strong work ethic, and set high standards for themselves and others. They are typically bored working for someone else and want to exert control over their environment.

- *Risk Tolerant.* They evaluate and manage calculated risks. They understand that accomplishing significant goals or innovative breakthroughs usually requires risk-taking, but they evaluate the probability and impact of risks and manage accordingly. They show courage in the face of uncertainty, and they distinguish internal feelings of anxiety from more objective measures of actual risk.

- *Confident.* They understand their own abilities and contribution, optimistically but realistically. They are not easily deterred by others' negativity or criticism, and they demonstrate high self-esteem and possess an internal locus of control, a belief that success will be due largely to their own initiative and efforts rather than to external forces or chance events.

- *Persuasive.* They appeal to others' motives and values by tuning in to the needs and interests of others and adapting their message and behavior to match.

- *Resilient.* They persistently work to overcome obstacles and do not allow setbacks to derail them. They persevere in the face of adversity.

- *Reliable/Focused.* They follow through, delivering on commitments to others, as well as to themselves. This is a foundational quality for execution, allowing a founder to gain traction and get things done. In most startup situations, this trait must be balanced with flexibility and openness (see "Conceptual") in order to adapt to new data and unfolding events.

- *People Oriented.* They value, understand, and leverage people. They possess strong social antennae and are gifted at working a room and building lasting relationships. This quality bundles together a number of related traits (amiability, extroversion, empathy, sociability, etc.) that are shaped and honed through early family and social life, as well as work experience.

- *Ethical.* They hold themselves to high personal and professional standards. Words and actions are aligned, forming the cornerstone for building trust and credibility with customers, team members, and partners.

How do you stack up against the list? If you are like 99 percent of startup founders, you possess some but not all of the above characteristics. This shouldn't deter you from pursuing your startup goals. Few entrepreneurs cover all the bases when it comes to the perfect entrepreneurial profile. But most highly successful founders understand who they are and how their personality matches up with the type and phase of startup they are launching. They then find and collaborate with people whose personalities and capabilities complement their own.

MAP YOUR SKILLS AND EXPERIENCE

Despite a few well-known examples of college dropouts who launch world-changing startups, entrepreneurial research supports the notion that the right kind of prior business experience, effectively applied, greatly enhances a founder's probability of success.[8] Even in the technology sector, widely assumed to be the domain of young, upstart entrepreneurs, data point to a strong link between experience and success. A 2009 Kauffman Foundation study entitled "Education and Tech Entrepreneurship" discovered that the majority of successful tech founders are "middle-aged, well educated in business or technical disciplines, with degrees from a wide assortment of schools. Twice as many United States–born tech entrepreneurs start ventures in their fifties as do those in their early twenties."[9]

Beyond bringing skills and relationships that will help you as an entrepreneur, the value of experience is primarily about pattern recognition. A person who has spent years in a particular industry can more quickly and accurately connect disparate data points into meaningful trends and opportunities, seeing cause and effect where others see only fog.

As with motivation, some types of experience are more beneficial than others. Map your own background and skills against the following six areas that prove valuable to almost any startup founder.

INDUSTRY, PROFESSIONAL, OR TECHNICAL EXPERIENCE THAT DIRECTLY RELATES TO YOUR CHOSEN STARTUP – What do you know how to do at the highest level? What can you do better than most everyone else? How does your *technical skill set relate to your new business?* Starting a business from scratch brings enough uncertainty and difficulty as it is without the added complication of learning an entirely new industry or discipline. When it comes to starting a new restaurant, I'll back the kitchen manager with ten years at Outback Steakhouse over the career attorney who loves to cook.

By the time they launched their first ventures, J.C. Faulkner and Mark Kahn had been working on the leading edges of their fields long enough to develop deep expertise and perspective. They understood their evolving industries, whose opinion to seek, and what questions to ask. They knew how to spot important trends and filter out irrelevant noise. By contrast, despite her twenty years of banking experience, Lynn Ivey was a rookie in the senior healthcare space. Her learning curve was a lot steeper than it would have been had she brought years of prior experience in the industry.

SALES AND MARKETING EXPERIENCE – The essence of business is the acquisition of customers, clients, and users. A founder who brings market-facing skills will enjoy a higher probability of success than a person who lacks these capabilities. Sales skills are best acquired through experience, ideally in the same industry as your new venture. But a strong track record of sales success in any industry implies that the founder brings an understanding of the importance of sales and all that it requires, as well as sales skills and habits that will transfer to new markets.

Early in the ascent of Modality, Mark Williams realized that growing his business would require a fundamental shift in his priorities and time allocation, away from product development and toward greater immersion in the market of prospective institutional clients and business partners. While Mark possessed a natural gift for relating to clients and partners—he's often the most intelligent, poised, and humble person in the room—he was unaccustomed to filtering and prioritizing sales leads or converting high-potential prospects into closed deals. He has diligently worked on this skill set as Modality has grown, but readily admits that an earlier tour of business-to-business sales and marketing would have benefited him and Modality greatly.

LEADERSHIP EXPERIENCE – A wide range of prior leadership roles can provide experience and learning that translate well to the needs of a new venture. Whether in a business setting or not, any role in which you have to get things done through others will test and refine your leadership skills.

At the same time, leadership roles in large businesses usually bring valuable learning experiences for future entrepreneurs. Every big company contains a wide spectrum of leaders and styles, some better suited than others for the startup world, but the skills required to utilize the talent and time of others in achieving higher level goals will serve a new entrepreneur well in almost any new venture setting.

As with other aspects of experience, only you can fully assess how well your prior leadership roles match up with your new venture challenge, guided by the questions: *Where have you led? What have you learned about how to lead? How well do these experiences transfer to your startup role, and in what ways can you best leverage your leadership strengths?*

GENERAL BUSINESS SEASONING AND EXPOSURE – Taking on a range of jobs early in a career almost always adds valuable business skills and perspective. "I was an English major in college," says Mark Kahn. "I spent a lot of time in different jobs at News Corp. and got to touch many sides of the business. I think I got a better kind of education than one might get at a business school. It was a very good place to get to learn something that I just wasn't really familiar with, to be honest with you. My father was a physician; my mother didn't work. It wasn't as though I was surrounded by business growing up, so it was my learning ground—and somebody paid me to do it, so that was a double bonus."

What skills have you learned through your work experience that will serve you well in your founding role? Valuable examples include:

- Negotiation (contracts, deals, etc.)

- Organization, planning, and project management

- Problem solving and decision making (critical thinking skills)

- Financial acumen (financial reporting, accounting, etc.)

- General technology skills and knowledge
- Networking and developing business relationships
- Effective communication and public speaking
- Interacting with and influencing senior executives

Whatever your skill set, identify significant gaps between your own capabilities and what your venture will require, and ask yourself: *Who has the necessary skills that I'm missing? Who might bring the pattern recognition that I don't possess?*

PAST ENTREPRENEURIAL EXPERIENCE – Many successful startups are launched by founders who have learned from prior entrepreneurial efforts, and a range of experiences qualify—being a member of a startup team, for example, or launching a new venture within a larger company. Both J.C. Faulkner and Mark Kahn started small businesses during college (a pizza parlor and a storage service, respectively). Although dealing with fewer zeros than in their later attempts, they gained invaluable experience for the future. Also, they both worked with or ran new ventures within their employer companies prior to making their startup leaps. When it comes to prior startup experience, success or failure is less important than the experience of going out on a limb, with something significant at stake, and making decisions in highly uncertain environments.

ADVERSITY – *What have been your toughest challenges, professionally and personally? How did you handle them? What did you learn from them and how might these lessons apply to your new venture?* Answers to questions like these can build your confidence and prepare you for the most challenging moments to come along your startup path.

Chris Holden continued to watch with interest as his former employee, Mark Kahn, built a series of specialized websites on the wild-west Web of the late 1990s. He recalls Mark's entrepreneurial adventure:

"He used his casino winnings to pull his team together, with no pay, and got the thing ready for prime time. One year into it, at the height of the dot-com bubble, he signed a deal with Martha Stewart's company OmniMedia. They were going to buy the business for $16 million and the deal was fully negotiated. He signs the contract and sends it back to them for counter-signature, and it was the day the bubble burst, spring of 2000. The CFO of OmniMedia calls him up and says, 'Hey, everything's fine. We're just going to sit on this. We're busy with some other stuff. The markets are doing weird things.' Long story short: They never signed the deal, and the whole thing crashed to zero. So, he had $16 million in hand, from his blackjack game to that point, then all to nothing."

Mark Kahn soldiered on. "Even during that time, we didn't say, 'Oh, the e-commerce market is blown up.' We tried to ride it out. We had 35 meetings (with VC firms), even though 35 said, 'No thank you.' You go to the next one and the next one and the next. That's what you have to do if you are committed to the business."

Unfortunately, the business ran out of money and stalled. Mark Kahn, needing to support a growing family, got a marketing job with another startup in New York City. Chris Holden joined a venture capital firm specializing in digital media investments and continued to watch with impressed fascination as his former colleague picked himself up and moved forward.

A few years later, when Mark Kahn had an idea for his next venture, to create an Internet marketplace bringing online advertisers and publishers together, Chris Holden brought his firm, Court Square Ventures, to the table with startup capital. He had seen Mark Kahn deal with crisis and failure and come out the other end as a stronger person. "Right now it's one of the most successful investments we've ever made," he says of TRAFFIQ, Mark's newest venture. "He plowed through his first failure, dusted himself off, and he did it again. And, he's so good at taking all the lessons he learned along the way and packaging them within himself. He truly is—I hate to be so extreme—but he's close to being the perfect entrepreneurial CEO."

To this point, our discussion of your readiness as a founder has focused on who you are, your motivation, personality, skills, and knowledge. The objective is not to be perfectly rounded in all areas—no founder will be—but to be well aware from the outset what you bring to the startup effort, where relevant gaps exist, and how to address those gaps. Consider the founder who plans to introduce a new technology into the medical field, bringing deep expertise in technology but no experience in healthcare. Clearly, she will benefit from working closely with partners who bring experience and relationships within the targeted medical markets. Or if an entrepreneur is highly conceptual and independent, but not very focused or socially inclined, he or she will likely thrive in product development and planning roles but may be less effective driving execution, leading teams, or building customer relationships. These are generalizations, so the key is that you apply the above questions to your specific situation to best align your strengths with the needs of your venture.

The realization that you don't have to be a superhero in all areas is tremendously liberating, as J.C. Faulkner discovered in building his founding team at D1. "One of our philosophies," he said, "was to exploit each other's strengths and forgive and shore up each other's weaknesses. We came to the conclusion that each of us doesn't have to be well rounded. The team has to be well rounded, but as individuals we don't have to be perfect."

LEVERAGE YOUR RELATIONSHIPS AND RESOURCES

Like every founder, you will bring a unique set of external connections and assets to your startup equation. Understanding how these match up with your startup goals and needs is a key step in getting your venture off on the right foot.

YOUR RELATIONSHIPS – *Who can help?* If you list the twenty, forty, or sixty-plus people (potential clients, family members, funders, team members, service partners, etc.) who might help you get your new business off the ground, I'll bet you can sort and filter that list down to a handful of absolutely essential relationships. These are *key relationships*—the vital few that must work well in order for you to succeed. A financial backer, a spouse, an indispensable sales manager, a well-connected client, a board chair, a father-in-law, any of these might be a key relationship that can make or break your startup. These relationships constitute your greatest points of leverage, meaning that they bring the highest upside, as well as the greatest risk (if they are not working well). As these relationships go, so goes your startup.

Who are your key relationships? What is the state of each key relationship? For each relationship that is not rock-solid, what do you need to do to solidify the relationship? Answering and acting on these questions is one of the powerful, though not always easy, ways to reduce your risk and elevate your probability of success.

At a broader level, you can expand and organize your entire brainstormed list, including anyone and everyone who might help you, buy from you, or need to know about you and your new venture. Think about prospective customers, employees, advisers, service partners, vendors, investors, and referral sources. Cast the widest net possible and cultivate a helpful network and community around your startup. Try to take an objective look at the shape of your wider network and target future relationship-building efforts to fill any major gaps.

YOUR RESOURCES – *What assets are available to you?* It's important to think through the type and amount of financial resources available to help launch your new venture and to provide an economic cushion until the business is generating healthy profits. These sources might include savings, existing or untapped lines of credit, physical assets that might be borrowed against, or interested investors waiting in the wings. In Chapter Five, I'll discuss the importance of tapping the right mix of financial resources in a way that aligns with your goals and needs to ensure your venture has enough funding to get off the ground.

POSITION YOURSELF FOR HIGH PERFORMANCE

Regardless of why you're starting a business and what skills and resources you bring, your performance as a founder will fluctuate from hour-to-hour and day-to-day. This is the nature of human striving. Some days are better than others. A key question for every startup founder is: *What does it mean to bring my very best, and what does this re-*

quire? After twenty years of studying high performance and coaching business leaders to achieve new levels of effectiveness, it's clear to me that most of us sit atop a deep well of energy and potential that is never fully tapped.

Honestly assessing your interests and needs in five domains— each of which can work in your favor, boosting your focus and performance, or work against you, diminishing or distracting your focus and performance—will help you to bring your best effort and energy to your startup challenge.

FINANCIAL NEEDS AND GOALS – *What minimum personal income do you need to earn on a monthly basis over the first twelve to thirty-six months to be able to pursue your venture? What are your longer-term personal financial goals in pursuing this venture?*

Most of us bring a minimum income need to our startup journey. As psychologist Abraham Maslow laid out in his *hierarchy of needs,*[10] unless and until our basic survival and safety needs are met, we won't give our full attention to higher goals and aspirations. If at all possible, take your income issue "off of the table" by identifying how much money you need to make during your startup process and then developing a game plan that will meet this need.

How you determine your income needs, and at what level you set them, is a highly personal decision that depends on many factors. The ideal scenario in launching a new business is to have minimal or no needs for near-term income, but this is rarely a sustainable situation. When he launched his first venture, Mark Kahn was prepared to operate for many months with no personal income. Several years later, when seeking funding for his second venture, he was in a different frame of mind. "Maybe it is both age and having kids and a family to support," he said, "but I made it clear to investors that I would be leaving a job that pays me well, and I needed to figure out how to finance the business up front so it worked for me on a personal level."

Longer-term financial goals are also important to identify. *Are you looking to reach a consistent, stable level of income over time? Are you hoping to create an exit event after five or ten years that represents a large payout to cover your early financial sacrifice and create financial independence going forward?* Your stance on these issues will frame your planning process and, more important, drive the sense of purpose and energy you bring to your founding role.

FAMILY SUPPORT AND ALIGNMENT – *How aware are family members or significant others of your plans for the new venture and what it will require? How supportive (confident, committed) are your family/significant others of this new venture? Who else are you counting on to support this venture? What is their level of support or resistance?*

I include in "family" any loved ones or significant others who are a consistent, important part of your life. The most common cases are husbands and wives and children, who inevitably bear some of your startup sacrifice and stress. I know of quite a few promising businesses that were abandoned because the founder's family was not adequately prepared for the stress or the risk associated with entrepreneurship. On the other side of the coin are people who achieve their startup goals but at a dramatic and painful cost. Tim Berry, founder of Palo Alto Software and bplans.com, has written, "Every class in entrepreneurship should have at least one session with somebody who got so obsessed with the business that they lost the rest of their life. It happens a lot."[11]

Typically, this is an area full of entrepreneurial selling and sugarcoating. You want your family members to believe in what you are doing, to have confidence in your new venture and the future you are making possible, and, of course, you want to minimize their anxiety about risks and challenges of entrepreneurship. But the realities and requirements of your new venture will quickly make their presence felt in your home, whether or not you prepare your family for them. Spouses caught unaware by financial crises and unexpected late nights at the office are much more likely to resist or panic than those who are looped in and consulted on the front end. So it's vital that you have honest and realistic conversations with family members about how the startup will affect or change your availability and schedule, how it will affect financial priorities, and how risks and challenges will be handled along the way. This includes listening closely to family members' concerns and fears and discussing how they can provide help and support. Don't underestimate the positive impact on your entrepreneurial performance that family support will bring or the added stress and strain that will arise if these issues go unexamined and unaddressed.

TIME AVAILABILITY AND COMMITMENT – *What current commitments of your time, other than your new venture, will remain in place? How many hours per week will be available for you to pursue your startup opportunity? How many hours per week do you expect to spend on this venture?*

The implications here are simple. Getting a new business off the ground takes time, a lot more time than most founders ever imagine. It always looks simpler on the back of a napkin than in everyday life. Your ability to drive your startup forward will strongly correlate to how much time and focus you can give to it. Paul Graham said it best, "Most founders of failed startups don't quit their day jobs, and most founders of successful ones do. If startup failure was a disease, the CDC would be issuing bulletins warning people to avoid day jobs."[12]

Realistically, many people are not in situations that allow them to put all of their time into getting their big idea off the ground, at least not initially. Some founders would rather be part-time entrepreneurs for lifestyle reasons. And your time availability will be driven partly by the first two domains: your income needs and your family circumstances. But understand that the amount of time you devote will impact how quickly you grow your business, what you need from other partners and stakeholders, and, ultimately, how you define and achieve success as an entrepreneur.

HEALTH AND PERSONAL CAPACITY – *What is the status of your physical/emotional health? How do you develop and sustain your capacity for productive work (e.g., exercise, nutrition, social and spiritual pursuits, etc.)?*

During more than a decade of working closely with senior executives to evaluate and improve their performance, I found that many of my clients had hit a wall of fatigue, stress, and resignation. They admitted that years of sixty- and seventy-hour workweeks had left them depleted. They were clearly not bringing their best selves to their work, but they saw no easy way out. The pipeline of challenges continued to flow at them with no break in sight.

In 2001, I began to share with clients a *Harvard Business Review* article, written by Jim Loehr and Tony Schwartz, titled "The Making of a Corporate Athlete."[13] The authors had successfully distilled a set of principles governing the sustained high performance of world-class athletes (Olympic champions, PGA golfers, and professional tennis players, for example) and applied these principles to challenges experienced by business leaders. Their fundamental premise, later captured in their best-selling book, *The Power of Full Engagement*, is that bringing your best self, your "A game," to any endeavor over a sustained period of time requires the systematic building of personal strength, stamina, and capacity on four basic levels: physical, mental, emotional, and spiritual (see the resources list in Appendix B for more detailed information and references about this model).[14] I found these concepts to be consistently helpful to clients and to myself and have further found that these ideas are wholly useful for new entrepreneurs, who are always seeking more energy, more time, greater focus, etc.

To maximize your impact as a founder, become a student of your own effectiveness and performance. *How do you manage and recover energy? Through what practices and activities do you refill your gas tank? How do you keep your mind sharp and uncluttered?* Although these questions may seem obvious, I rarely encounter a new founder who couldn't elevate his or her personal impact and performance by improving personal "care and feeding." In addition to boosting your venture's odds of success, these steps will add to your quality of life and work. Simply put, you'll get more enjoyment out of your startup ride.

TRANSITION – *What aspects of your prior identity or role will serve you well in your new venture? What aspects do you want to leave behind or will hinder you in some way? What unfinished business do you need to wrap up in order to fully focus on your new venture, without distraction or doubt?*

You can't live your former life and move in a new direction at the same time. Your former life includes obligations, affiliations, contracts, responsibilities, and personal habits. Of course, some of these will remain unchanged, but it is impossible to bring your full energy to a new venture until you make a clean break from prior roles and obligations that don't align with your entrepreneurial goals. This usually involves tough choices. You want to stay involved in your golf group or continue to have breakfast every Friday with friends from your former job, but these will steal time away from the priorities of your startup. You want to be included in social events and fishing trips, take in concerts, and keep your spot on the neighborhood council. And you want to hang on to those favorite clients that you've had for years, who are lucrative but not aligned with how you need to spend time in building your new business.

William Bridges, in his classic book, *Transitions*, asserts that every new beginning starts with endings.[15] Over decades of working with thousands of people, struggling to navigate major changes in their lives (e.g., divorce, job loss, or death of a loved one), he noticed that the concrete, external changes in our lives—moving into a new house or office, for example, or driving to a new work location—are easily absorbed by most people. What usually trips us up or holds us back is the thicket-like process of *inner* transition, where we hold on to expectations, beliefs, or attitudes that are relics of the past. The key to marshalling your energy for the future is to acknowledge what needs to be laid to rest, finish any unfinished business, and don't look back.

Purifying Your Entrepreneurial Passion

As I mentioned earlier in this chapter, avoiding the passion trap doesn't require that you suppress your enthusiasm or commitment. Instead, the solution lies in elevating and focusing your positive energy, creating a more pure, potent, and sustainable brand of passion. Your startup idea deserves no less.

Here are four principles for purifying your startup passion, while also avoiding the dangers it might bring: *understand it, connect it, strengthen it,* and *direct it.*

UNDERSTAND YOUR PASSION

When I was nine or ten years old, I remember telling my dad that I had butterflies in my stomach before a little league football game. "That's okay," he said. "It means you're excited, and you want to do

your best." Those words shifted me from anxiety to positive antici-
pation. I felt that if I put my best foot forward and had a good time,
everything would turn out well. My father had put a useful frame
around the energy I had inside, and that made all the difference.

As you chase your big idea, here are three strategies for putting a
useful frame around your passion and energy:

1. *Clarify your reasons and goals.* Get clear on why you want to
   start a business and how these motivations will influence your
   startup plan and approach.

2. *Distinguish the fire in your belly from the weight on your
   shoulders.* The first feeling comes from true passion, a can't-
   wait-to-get-out-of-bed feeling, while the second is one of obligation and compliance. You will feel some of each as an
   entrepreneur. Look for roles that maximize the fire and minimize the weight.

3. *Understand what you bring to the table.* Acknowledge and accept your personality, skills, and motivations, all of the dimensions of founder readiness outlined earlier in this
   chapter. This self-awareness will drive your healthy and skillful use of entrepreneurial passion.

CONNECT YOUR PASSION

Business is personal. We all want to personally connect to the work
we do. Many of our strongest drives—to create, to achieve, to relate,
to make a difference—play out in the arena of work. The fact that
business is personal is the very reason many of us choose to become
entrepreneurs in the first place. It's the reason employees leave large,
impersonal companies to join new ventures. It allows us to connect
our startup passion with people who share it or support it. Approaches for connecting your passion are:

- *Personalize business.* In building D1, J.C. Faulkner used rituals and practices to create a workplace that valued and high-
  lighted the personal nature of work. As an example, he paid
  for professionally photographed portraits of all headquarters

employees' children and loved ones, giving copies of the portraits to each employee for their home use. In addition, every
portrait was hung along a prominent hallway in the headquarters building, creating a mosaic of the faces most important
to the hundreds of people who worked in the home office. It
was a poignant reminder of *why* most of them came to work
every day. This became a touchstone of the culture and added
perspective and depth to interactions in the building.

- *Enhance your team's alignment and readiness.* Keep in mind
  that the principles of founder readiness apply not only to
  you, but to everyone else on your team as well. Bob Tucker,
  J.C. Faulkner's business attorney, recalls J.C.'s awareness of
  this fact. "He once told me," Bob says, "that he wanted the
  people on his management team to never have felt smarter,
  to never have felt more confident or more capable than they
  were in their D1 jobs. Anything and everything that could be
  done to achieve that outcome he wanted to do."

- *Find "your people."* This useful concept comes from Pamela
  Slim, author of *Escape from Cubicle Nation,* who has built her
  thriving consulting, coaching, and writing practice by attracting people who share her passion and not losing sleep over
  people who don't.[16]

STRENGTHEN YOUR PASSION

Here are four strategies for fueling a healthy, sustainable enthusiasm
for your new venture:

1. *Clear your way.* Free up energy by relinquishing old obligations or time-wasters that no longer align with your startup
   priorities.

2. *Feed your curiosity.* Learn everything you can about your
   business concept, the markets you are entering, and the players and competitors in the industry. The more you learn, the
   more confidence and energy you will bring to your founding
   role.

3. *Refill your tank.* Pay attention to how you perform, how you recover, what renews you, and what depletes you. Based on these observations, build regular routines and rituals to continually strengthen your energy and performance.

4. *Welcome adversity.* In startups, as in life, we cannot predict the future, nor can we fully protect ourselves from the challenges and crises to come. Adversity can strengthen an entrepreneur and a team like no other force, especially when approached with the attitude captured by German diplomat and psychotherapist Karlfried Von Durkheim, who said, "Only to the extent that a man exposes himself over and over again to annihilation, can that which is indestructible arise within him. In this lies the dignity of daring."[17]

DIRECT YOUR PASSION

Finally, aim your passion in ways that will reduce the danger of falling into the passion trap and increase your overall odds of venture success. For example, cultivate:

- Passion for your customer, rather than your product
- Passion for learning the truth, rather than being right
- Passion for exploring contradictory data, rather than holding on to old beliefs
- Passion for learning about your competitors' strengths, rather than dismissing them
- Passion for finding and attracting the best possible talent for your venture team

CHAPTER FOUR

The Pull of the Market

Attach to Your Customer, Not to Your Idea

"The greatest danger for a new venture is to 'know better' than the customer what the product or service should be."

—Peter Drucker, *Innovation and Entrepreneurship*

Apple founder Steve Jobs predicted its impact on society would rival that of the personal computer. Its inventor, Dean Kamen, believed cities and towns would be redesigned around it. "It will be to the car," he said, "what the car was to the horse-and-buggy." And legendary venture capitalist John Doerr promised that its maker would be the fastest company in history to reach a billion dollars in sales.[1]

In December 2001, in one of the most anticipated launches in commercial history, Kamen and his backers unveiled the Segway Personal Transporter, a revolutionary alternative to walking or driving. The two-wheeled, magically balancing Segway was a technological marvel, ten years and $100 million in the making, and it had wowed riders in super-secret tests. A gleaming production facility sat ready to crank out as many as 40,000 units every month in hopes that city dwellers across the world would embrace the product as a solution for congested traffic, overcrowded parking lots, and long, exhausting walks.

But urban commuters never got the memo. After seven years and more than $250 million in invested capital, the Segway had yet to catch on with its intended market. Only about 25,000 Segways had been sold *in total* by 2008, mostly for police, security, and industrial use. As *BusinessWeek* noted in 2006, "the problem that he (Kamen) wanted to solve, the need for a clean, energy efficient vehicle that could coexist with pedestrians and replace the car in the world's cities, was one that others didn't see."[2] For most urbanites, the Segway seemed no more practical than the bicycle, a tried-and-true device invented two centuries ago and available at a fraction of the cost, prompting the *Washington Post* to dub it "The Invention That Runs on Hype."[3]

But don't count out Segway just yet. During his tenure as CEO from 2005 to 2010, James D. Norrod pushed the company to expand its foothold in the police, security, and industrial markets, maintaining that "market development is about finding one market that works really well and building your business from there." The company has also explored new applications for its Smart Motion technology, including robotics, toys, unmanned military vehicles, and the development of four-wheeled, multiperson prototypes. For Norrod, these approaches have been the result of listening to what the market has to say. "If people want four wheels," he said, "I should give 'em four wheels."[4]

The Segway story is one dramatic example of a nearly universal experience among new business founders and investors. What at first seems like a slam-dunk business idea is usually an approximation, a first stab at something you hope will resonate with paying customers. You won't know for sure until real customers buy and use your product. Or not.

Most often, identifying the right market means refining, adapting, even reinventing your original concept. Apple, Yahoo, and Google were not their founders' first ideas. Chris Holden, referring to the successful startups his venture capital firm has funded, says that "none of them looks identical to what we thought we were investing in." Two of history's most celebrated entrepreneurs, Bill Gates and Paul Allen, first started a company called Traf-O-Data but later saw the tremendous market potential for a different business, something they named Microsoft.

Like Dean Kamen and many others with inspired ideas, these entrepreneurs learned a powerful lesson: An idea isn't great until the market says it is.

Developing a Strong Market Orientation

Of all the factors that can help you get your business off the ground, the most important will be the presence of a ready market, which can be defined as a sufficient number of actual (versus potential) customers who will pay, right now, for a product or service. There is no room for abstraction on this simple point. Truly superior business concepts always translate into living, breathing customers who will pull out their wallets and hand over hard-earned money. Everything else is a warm-up.

This is why hard work, cool technology, lots of funding, or superior talent won't, by themselves, guarantee startup success. In fact, if the market is right, these attributes might not even be necessary. A founder with questionable skills, little money, and a B-grade product might still launch a business by stumbling into a white-hot market, which can disguise and cure a lot of ills. When J.C. Faulkner built D1 into one of the strongest mortgage companies in the United States, during the late 1990s, he knew that some of his competitors made money only because of a booming market. "When running downhill," he would say, "everybody thinks they're an athlete." He wanted his team to be ready for the inevitable market downswing, and when it came, D1 swiftly outran its competitors.

As a passionate founder, you must wrestle with a paradox. Passion is an inner force, driving you from the inside out. But the surest way to get a new venture off the ground is to build it from the *outside in*, allowing market forces to pull and shape your idea into a thriving business. As we saw in Chapter Two, your attachment to a cool business concept can amplify your inner world of belief and optimism so much that you lose your objectivity about the needs, desires, and fears of prospective customers and move forward with a product that nobody wants.

The best possible antidote is to bring a strong market orientation to your new venture. A market orientation will immunize you against one of the most dangerous effects of the passion trap: your blind faith that customers will believe in your product simply because *you* do. And although it won't guarantee that you'll immediately find the perfect market for your idea, a healthy market orientation will dramatically improve your odds of finding a ready base of customers to sustain your startup.

What is a market orientation? I've found that market-oriented entrepreneurs do three things to ensure that their passion connects with ample opportunity:

1. *They obsessively* emphasize *the market and the customer.* This is a mindset issue. *How do you think about your business relative to the customers you serve? Are you determined to build your business from the outside in? Are you starting with the market, and developing your business from there, or are you a "product in search of a market"?*

2. *They strive to* know *their markets and customers.* *How fully do you understand your customers, their needs and preferences, and the problems you are solving for them? How will you continue to improve your knowledge over time?*

3. *They* execute *on the market opportunity.* *How will you successfully market and sell your offerings? What kind of sales engine is required for success? Do you really understand how customers experience your products and services, and what kind of value is created for them?*

Through the rest of this chapter, I will further define these three strategies to ensure that you find and connect with customers who are just as passionate about your offerings as you are. Then, I'll share a set of questions for giving your startup idea a *market scrub* to scrutinize your concept in the bright light of the marketplace.

EMPHASIZE YOUR MARKET

The next time you're in line at a fast food-restaurant or a corner drugstore, pay attention to the transaction happening in front of you. *Do you see a product being sold or a human need being met? Do you see a hamburger or hunger? A bottle of Ibuprofen or a spouse at home with a killer headache?*

How you see the world of commerce will govern how you design, build, and run your startup. Whether you see the world as products or as needs is vitally important. We live in an increasingly consumer- and technology-driven culture, and we love stuff: gadgets, widgets, technologies, and things. Most of us, most of the time, "see" products and services when we look at a business.

But every successful offering corresponds to a need it was designed to meet. Products and needs are inseparable. To continually remind myself of this, I keep a shabby hand-drawn rendering of the classic figure-ground illusion (see Figure 4-1) taped to my office wall.

Figure 4-1. The figure-ground illusion.

In the picture, I see the white vase as my product or service. It represents my great idea, my "baby." Of course, as I continue looking, foreground and background will shift, revealing two faces in profile.

These are the faces of the customers who shape my product, the markets that give life to any business. Whether I notice them or not, they are always there.

Emphasizing your market means continually seeing the faces, never losing sight of the market's absolute power over your business, despite force of habit drawing your attention back to the vase, again and again. Focus on your market, the wellspring of any healthy business, and you can be confident that the right products and services will emerge over time.

Stacy's Pita Chips would never have been born if its founders had clung to their original business idea or if they had overlooked an unexpected market need standing, literally, right in front of them. In the mid-1990s, Stacy Madison, a Boston social worker, dreamed of opening a health food restaurant. With very little money, she and her business partner, Mark Andrus, decided to start with a small sandwich cart in downtown Boston, selling all-natural pita-wrap sandwiches. Hungry customers were soon forming long lines down the block. To keep them interested while they waited, Stacy and Mark served them seasoned pita chips baked from leftover pita bread. Customers flipped over the chips, convincing Stacy and Mark to package them for sale in stores. Before long, the retail chip business took off, so they abandoned their restaurant plans and pursued the pita chip idea full-time. In 2006, having achieved more than $60 million in annual sales, Stacy's Pita Chips was acquired by Frito-Lay, the world's largest snack food company. Not bad for a lunch-cart business, and all possible because Stacy and Mark put their attention where it belonged, on a customer need.[5]

The idea of placing emphasis on market needs is hardly revolutionary, but it is easier said than done, especially among technologists and product developers. Paul Graham knows this as well as anyone. Through Y Combinator, his seed-stage technology venture fund, he invites a wide array of ideas from very young, mostly brilliant software engineers, hoping to launch the next Google or Facebook. Graham says that a lot of funding requests come from "promising people with unpromising ideas," so he and his colleagues have settled on a four-word mantra for what makes a technology stick: *Make something people want*. It permeates every Y Combinator program and is printed on T-shirts given to startup teams. "If you had to reduce the recipe for a successful startup to four words," Graham says, "those would probably be the four."[6]

KNOW YOUR MARKET

Anyone who has played Pin the Tail on the Donkey can understand the challenge of launching a new product or service. You're blindfolded and reaching forward, hopefully closing in on your target but with no way of knowing for sure. The kids who did well in that childhood game always had parents who grabbed their shoulders and lined them up in the right direction. The rest of us blindly wandered halfway across the house.

Knowing your market is like having someone grab you by the shoulders and point you in the right direction. Although you're flying somewhat blind, your odds of finding a robust market go up dramatically. The reason is simple: Your ability to meet customer needs is strongly correlated to how well you understand them.

In 2005, American companies spent over a trillion dollars a year on outbound marketing, representing almost 10 percent of the country's gross domestic product. If it were a vertical industry, marketing would rank as the country's fifth largest, behind manufacturing, government, real estate, and professional services.[7] The primary purpose of all this activity is to broadcast product messages out to as many prospective customers as possible. Seth Godin, in his 2005 book, *All Marketers Are Liars*, wrote that "all marketing is about telling stories . . . painting pictures that they (customers) choose to believe."[8]

Granted, storytelling can be a powerful tool, but it is not the essence of business. A more essential issue is whether a business creates *actual* value for customers, rather than expected or perceived value, the kind created by marketing impressions. A story won't determine how well you solve customer problems or whether the market is ultimately satisfied or frustrated with your product. Your customer's experience of your product, not the stories they hear about it, will make or break your business.

This is why, for a new venture, the first and most vital aspect of marketing is the *inbound* part, the process of listening to the marketplace, learning about customers, and hearing their individual and collective voices. This will be an ongoing, iterative process. What you "know" may be proven wrong, and even well understood markets will change over time. But you can dramatically improve your odds of a solid start—and avoid some major headaches—by understanding the market you are going after.

To keep it simple, there are three basic paths to getting market knowledge before you launch. You can bring it with you. You can learn it. Or you can hire it.

BRING IT – When it comes to really knowing a customer base, there's no substitute for direct market experience. I'll always bet on founders who have worked for years in their targeted industry, especially if that includes field roles in marketing or sales, versus those who are new to a market or who have spent no time in the field.

I've already noted the value of J.C. Faulkner's experience prior to founding D1, and every bit of that experience was centered in the marketplace. Over the first ten years of his business career, he took on branch sales jobs throughout the United States, developing broad industry relationships and learning about the market's cyclical nature and fluctuating rates. In his last corporate assignment before his startup leap, he immersed himself even more deeply in the market, leading a two-year internal venture to evaluate and buy loans from other mortgage lenders across the country. "In order to work with these lenders," J.C. says, "I had to go in and get their financials and understand their operations. I studied fifty of these shops over a two-year period, and spent a lot of time with all of them. After a while, I knew them better than they knew themselves."

J.C. then designed his new venture to out-compete the businesses he had studied. Because of his relationships and credibility across the industry, he attracted top talent to run his first sales branches. Right away, he and his new team exceeded their sales projections, breaking even within nine months.

D1 was born in the market. The very idea of the company came not from a product development lab, but rather from its founder's sales experience, his relationships within an industry, and his ability to see a phenomenal opportunity in the making. From inception, his venture was tightly nested within a known market space.

LEARN IT - Starting a successful business is a non-stop learning process, most of which happens after you're up and running. But you can improve your odds of a solid start, and avoid some major headaches, by doing your market homework before you start. Studies have shown that effective market analysis can prevent up to 60 percent of startup failures.[9]

How you collect data, and how much you collect, will depend on the type, scale, and complexity of your startup; how much time and money are available; how much you already know; and so on.

The simplest way to learn about a market is the old-fashioned way. Get out and talk to people whose opinions you trust: potential customers, industry colleagues, and respected competitors. Ask people what they are seeing in the market, how their needs and interests are changing, and what problems and opportunities they are dealing with. Focus on *listening* to them rather than selling your idea and use their input to reevaluate your product or service. While enhancing your market knowledge, this approach also creates interest in your new business. These conversations plant seeds for future sales and referrals. Build a database of these contacts so that you can keep them informed of your progress as you move forward.

Another informal way to learn about your market is through published sources. Read as much relevant information as you can: industry magazines, research reports, customer databases, census information, etc. The Web is an increasingly broad and deep source of market information (see Appendix B for a list of good starting points for online market research), although the accuracy and quality of Web-based information can be difficult to verify. Plenty of fee-based services are available to provide more reliable market information on sectors most critical to your business plan.

To ensure that you don't bend the data to fit your preconceptions, hearing what you want to hear, involve others in your information-gathering efforts. A talented marketing consultant can conduct surveys or focus groups in a more detached manner than you, and these professionals can research available data more efficiently, unfettered by your hopes and biases. They can also help you overcome the fact that customers aren't always able to articulate their deeper motivations. They will say they prefer low-calorie ice cream then take the high-cal stuff home in their shopping bag.

One more word about learning in advance: Don't overdo it. In the absence of real customers, your data collection will reach a point of diminishing returns. Be sure to do your homework and examine your beliefs about the market you are about to enter, but save a healthy chunk of your time, money, and energy for the rich learning that will come only after your products are out there and the clock is running. In Chapter Six, I'll explore more thoroughly how to set up feedback and learning loops after you launch to continuously build a better understanding of your customer base and your overall market.

HIRE IT - If you don't have direct experience in your target market, consider hiring or partnering with somebody who does. In his study of 850 technology startups, Edward Roberts of MIT found that "companies that had a marketing person or salesperson at the beginning did better than those that did not. Having a marketing or salesperson (with specific industry expertise) as a cofounder seems to be critical."[10] If you can find the right person—an important "if"—you can add immediately valuable market expertise to your team, freeing you to focus your energy in areas where you are more likely to shine.

Another approach is to tap an outside sales adviser or marketing consultant on a temporary basis. You can scale the role to meet your specific needs without committing a full salary or giving up ownership in your business. More than ever, because of macro-economic challenges, a lot of highly talented marketing and sales professionals are on the sidelines, acting as free agents, available to help startups better understand their markets. As a bonus, if the person is a great fit, you can opt to bring him or her on board full-time down the road.

EXECUTE ON YOUR MARKET OPPORTUNITY

In his 1987 book, *Moments of Truth,* Jan Carlzon tells the story of how he reinvigorated his ailing company, the Swedish Air Service (SAS), by focusing his 20,000 employees on the customer experience. His logic was straightforward: The airline served 10 million customers a year. Each customer came into contact with approximately five SAS employees during the year, and each contact lasted an average of 15 seconds. He wrote, "The SAS is 'created' 50 million times a year, 15 seconds at a time. These 50 million 'moments of truth' are the moments that ultimately determine whether SAS will succeed or fail as a company."[11]

More than twenty years later, this notion still cuts to the heart of what makes any business viable and enduring. Carlzon was operating a large service organization, but the idea that businesses are the sum of their customers' experiences perfectly applies to founders of seed-stage startups, whether they are hawking websites, widgets, or accounting services. The global economic crisis of 2008, and the fact that it was caused by bubbles and run-ups largely empty of assumed value, returned us even more squarely back to fundamentals. Underneath all the noise and clutter that can accompany your startup process, it's helpful to remember a simple truth: If you create enough value for enough paying customers, much of your initial risk melts away.

When your product or service is ready for prime time, here are five guidelines for gaining an early edge in the marketplace.

1. *Invest to acquire customers.* By "invest," I don't mean spend wads of cash, unless you're a well-capitalized founder with a clear-headed plan calling for that. I am suggesting that you put other assets to use, including the most precious resources available to you: your focus, time, and energy. Are you directing these toward generating prospects, converting them into paying customers, and stoking the sales engine to build a longer-term revenue stream? Or are you hoping that customers will flock to your better mousetrap simply because of its magical, magnetic pull?

I sought much advice when I started out as an independent consultant. One piece that stuck with me came from a legend in my field, who, in an interview, was asked to name the secret that distinguishes successful consultants from the rest. He thought for a moment, then he replied, "clients." Although most new founders understand the importance of building a healthy pipeline of clients, they also routinely underestimate what's required to do it, even with a well-targeted offering.

Revenue is a lagging indicator. Your customer count will be a function of how much time, attention, and, as necessary, money you put into your marketing and sales efforts. The look and feel of your particular approach will depend on your business model and plan, who you are targeting, through what channels, etc., which I'll discuss in more detail in Chapter Five. Whatever your plan for acquiring customers, be sure not to take short cuts in this vital area.

2. *Go for game-changing partnerships.* A common theme among successful entrepreneurs is that they don't attempt to do it all themselves. They create early alliances that bring stability, customers, connections, capacity, or promotional support. Whether it's that first monster client account or a highly trafficked website that features your product on its home page, big-ticket partnerships can radically alter the growth trajectory of your business. Microsoft was essentially born through a deal to provide the operating system for IBM's first personal computer. Modality's first big break came as a result of Mark Williams's hard-earned partnership with Apple.

As David Thompson notes in his book, *Blueprint to a Billion,* these alliances are often highly asymmetric, with the larger, more established partner holding all of the power.[12] Such partnerships bring challenges and risks. You can become overly dependent on a single mammoth partner, for example, or lose direct contact with your end user. Making the right alliances work in your favor will call for boldness, creativity, persistence, and strong relationship skills.

As you look across your market, use these questions as guidelines for identifying and landing game-changing alliances:

- Who currently has relationships with your target customers?

- Who do you currently view as a competitor that, if approached differently, could be a useful partner?

- What early customers would instantly connect you with other prospective customers or elevate your business profile in a positive way?

- What can you offer each prospective partner and vice versa? Where are the win-win opportunities linking your business concept and theirs?

- What specific steps can you take to explore and strengthen the most promising relationships?

3. *Understand your user's experience.* There's nothing like the feeling of making that first sale and serving that first customer. Your effort and sacrifice have borne real fruit. So cash that check, whether for $16 or $16,000, and pop the champagne.

But, after the celebration, remember that early sales don't always equate to satisfied customers. First-time buyers may flock to you because of the novelty effect of your new product (think of how much traffic most restaurants attract in their first few weeks). Now that real customers are involved, you can begin to answer some vital questions: How effectively are you solving your customers' problems? Are you creating real value for them? Are they the right customers for you? If so, will they buy from you again and refer other customers to you? Answering questions like these will help you build a sustainable market presence over time.

4. *Focus and go deep with the right opportunities.* The early stages of a startup are all about opening up, experimenting, and

generating possibilities. It's the time to throw your best stuff out there and see what sticks. But as leads turn into viable market opportunities, many startups reach a point where experimentation is no longer necessary or helpful. To propel the business forward, you must choose, focus, and execute in a few core areas. This often means saying no to some exciting options, a fact that can severely test founders accustomed to saying yes to any potential revenue source. If the yes-habit isn't broken, you're likely to stretch yourself too thin and fail to make a major impact with any one initiative.

The challenge is in knowing which opportunities to pursue more deeply, and which ones to avoid. Here are a few guiding questions:

- How well does the opportunity align with your purpose, your plan, and your passion?

- How will it impact cash flow? Will it yield an immediate return of cash, or will it function as a short-term investment with lagging return?

- What is the degree of difficulty? How well does it match up with your strengths?

- What will you have to give up to successfully take it on? To what will you say "no" to free up capacity for this "yes"?

- What are the costs/risks to you if this opportunity doesn't work out as planned? Are these acceptable and manageable?

5. *If you face a revenue crisis, treat it like one.* Falling short of early sales goals is the rule rather than the exception among startups. Usually, these initial shortfalls are not as dangerous as another common phenomenon: the unsettling tendency of founding teams to deny that things may not be going well, to avoid talking about it, and to rationalize away the possible implications. This well-worn path of denial, most acute

among passionate, true believers, often delays or obscures critical learning, choices, and actions. In the interest of "staying positive," founding teams allow the enterprise to sink more deeply into a hole.

Here are a few guidelines for monitoring and reacting to early sales news.

Don't:

- Avoid looking at financial data (this is surprisingly common, like leaving personal 401K statements unopened during a market free-fall).

- Shield key partners, investors, or co-founders from disappointing news, as this only ensures they will not be able to help.

- Implement a knee-jerk response without understanding what is causing low sales.

- Wait for changes in some external circumstance over which you have no control, such as economic recovery.

Do:

- Look at sales information frequently and closely.

- Take bad signs seriously, *before* they grow into crises.

- Discuss any deviations from your game plan openly with key partners and investors.

- Investigate and analyze until you understand why sales are low (see Appendix B for Eric Ries's simple but powerful process for finding and addressing root cause: "The Five Whys").

- Take appropriate action.

When assessing causes, try to distinguish internal process issues that can be corrected (such as product errors, communication gaps, or distribution snags) from more fundamental issues that cannot be summarily fixed (such as significant, unanticipated shifts in the marketplace). The former circumstance calls for quick, focused action, whereas the latter calls for a big picture reevaluation of your overall business model and approach. In some cases, early sales shortfalls are a canary in the coal mine, an advance signal that the market for your idea is too weak to support a profitable business. If you can grasp this possibility early enough, you'll have a healthy head start on redirecting your assets and capabilities to a more welcoming opportunity.

Antidote to the Passion Trap: Give Your Idea a Market Scrub

The best way to protect yourself from attachment to a nonviable business idea is to scrutinize your concept through a market lens. The five sets of questions below will force you to take a market-oriented look at your product or service and better understand your prospective customer base. (This is a simplified list taken from a more thorough set of market-oriented questions contained in the "Startup Readiness Tool" in Appendix A.)

Most likely, these questions will be hard to answer on your first pass. They are designed to provoke scrutiny and analysis of your idea, to lessen your danger of falling into the passion trap and, ultimately, to improve your odds of finding fertile ground for your business idea. Try to develop a well-thought-out perspective on each of the following questions, understanding that your answers will shift over time as you begin to grow your customer base.

1. *What basic need or problem are you addressing? What is your value proposition to the customer?* Lynn Ivey personally experienced the confusion, worry, and frustration that families feel as they try to care for loved ones struggling with cognitive dementia. By providing a "home away from home," during the daytime hours, The Ivey would give family caregivers much needed relief and peace of mind and provide ailing seniors with high-quality care and stimulation. Lynn's clear identification of an acute need was a great starting point, but her challenge would lie in convincing her target audience

that her solution was superior to other alternatives and in catching families at the right time, when frustration and worry were great enough to merit The Ivey's cost and a change from the status quo.

In thinking about the need you are addressing, ask yourself: Are you offering a "pain pill" or a "vitamin?" Pain pills are products or services that solve an acute user problem and alleviate anxiety, fear, or frustration. Plumbers, tow-trucks, and hospital emergency rooms are in the pain resolution business. Vitamins are products that customers view as nice to have, rather than absolutely essential. Upgrading your computer's processing speed would function as a vitamin for most users, whereas rescuing a crashed hard drive is a pain pill.

The conventional wisdom among marketing professionals is that vitamins are harder to sell than pain pills, but this is not a hard and fast rule. Many successful products and services appeal to higher-level motivations, for excitement, pleasure, or self-improvement, for example. But the more clearly you understand the nature of the value you are attempting to provide, as seen and experienced by the customer, the more effectively you can position and sell your solution.

2. *Who is your core customer?* Starbucks Coffee's impressive growth over the years has been driven, in part, by the company's ability to segment and understand its customers. Starbucks knows that those customers it calls "Super Regulars" comprise 4 percent of all visitors, while generating 20 percent of total revenue. They know that "Coffee House Enthusiasts" are younger coffee drinkers, who are aligned with Starbucks's core values and bring the greatest future spending potential. When Starbucks planners are evaluating a new idea or initiative, one basic litmus test is whether the change will appeal to Super Regulars and Coffee House Enthusiasts. If not, the discussion often moves on.[13]

As a startup, you can only aspire to Starbucks's high level

of customer understanding, but you can ask the right questions to identify your early market "sweet spot," that market segment where customer demand for your offerings is likely to be greatest. Start at the simplest level and work from there. Who is most impacted by the problem you are solving? Who is already using your product or something like it? What's motivating them to use it? How would you describe those who seem like the best fit for your offerings and why?

3. *What is the nature of the overall market opportunity?* This question gets at the longer-term viability and growth potential for your new business. You can solve acute problems for an initial set of buyers but fail to find enough of them to grow, or even sustain, your business over time. Markets have characteristics and personalities just as people do. They can be young or old; large or small; steady or volatile; wide or narrow. In evaluating your market opportunity, and the broader forces acting upon it, consider at least three dimensions: size, context, and timing.

With regard to size, ask yourself: *How large is your target market? How fast is it growing (or declining)? Why is it growing (or declining)? Is it emerging or mature? Is it poised for boom or bust?*

When founded, both Modality and The Ivey were entering growth industries with distinct profiles. Mark Williams's decision to develop applications for the iPhone in 2007 put him on the cusp of an explosive wave of growth in the mobile learning markets worldwide. Lynn Ivey, when she launched her center in 2007, was also catering to a population on the rise, the aging baby boomer generation, although the growth curve for this "age wave" has followed a slower, steadier climb. In fact, Lynn Ivey's vision for an upscale, full-service adult daycare facility may have been launched well ahead of its time, perhaps by five to ten years.

Concerning context, ask yourself: *What's happening in your industry? What larger forces and trends are driving your opportunity (economic, technological, demographic, social, regulatory, environmental, etc.)?*

Modality was riding on the back of a technological sea-change, the irreversible movement of computing power onto mobile devices and a population of learners increasingly hungry for higher-quality content accessible at more times and in more places. As we will see in Chapter Six, this broader trend would lead to new categories of revenue opportunities for Modality, reaching beyond its initial direct-to-consumer product line.

As for timing, ask yourself: *How long will your window of opportunity be open? Why is now the right time to enter the market?*

Mark Williams and his team assumed that their early-to-market advantage would be brief—they referred to it as a "fifteen-second lead"—and they knew competitors would quickly attempt to duplicate their early success with health-care education titles. But no one fully predicted the explosion of competitive products that filled Apple's online channel soon after the release of its iPhone Software Developer Kit. By the end of 2009, 100,000 applications would be available to users of iPhone and iPod Touch. Modality's window of opportunity had, indeed, been narrow. Had the company waited a few additional months to launch, its first products would never have stood out in the long, noisy line of competitors.

4. *Who else is currently addressing (or attempting to address) the opportunity, and how? Why do you think the opportunity is not yet fully exploited?* The tendency to underrate or dismiss the competition is one of the most common, and dangerous, characteristics of passionate entrepreneurs. The remedy is simple: Take inventory of the relevant players in your chosen market space, and do your homework to understand their strategies, strengths, and weaknesses. Tools for analyzing competitive forces abound, but your willingness to explore the competitive landscape with curiosity and objectivity is more critical than the particular tool used. Seek to understand what is happening in your target market space, being careful not to downplay the strengths of competitors in your market. Also, include in your evaluation *any* alternatives that serve to satisfy the customer problem you are targeting, even if those alternatives don't appear to be direct competitors.

One of the effects of Lynn Ivey's passion for her solution was underestimating the power of two competitive forces at play in her chosen market. The first was the home care industry, which had grown significantly over the prior decade as a result of the same aging trend spotlighted by Lynn. Several home care companies had been entrenched in the local market for years, providing in-home skilled nurses and companions for frail and declining seniors. Although these services were defined as "competition" in Lynn's first business plan, she actually thought of them as important partners and referral sources, rather than competitors. She hoped they would send prospects to The Ivey who weren't a good fit for in-home care or bring their own clients to the center for socially stimulating field trips. As she looks back at the sales challenges of her first two years of operation, it's clear that in-home care was a favored solution for many of her "ideal" client prospects. A second competitive alternative to The Ivey was the simple, powerful force of inertia, the tendency for a family's status quo situation to maintain itself. Even when family members saw The Ivey as a potential solution for their worries, the complications of switching their loved one into a new routine seemed to outweigh the perceived benefits.

5. *What is your competitive advantage? What is unique about your offering (your "secret sauce")? What differentiates you in the eyes of customers?* When Professor Karl Ulrich of Wharton Business School opens his undergraduate product-design class each semester, he rolls into the classroom atop a Segway Personal Transporter. After fielding comical looks from students and offering each of them an opportunity to ride the device, he uses the Segway as a case of an inspired and creative product that has yet to find its ideal user. Beyond the

obvious point that the brilliance of a product's design doesn't always translate into customers, he contends that the basic market challenge for the Segway is that, although it is potentially handy for a range of potential users (commuters, security guards, golfers, etc.) it's not the *best* solution for any of them. In other words, each type of potential user has a more favorable alternative, one that out-competes the Segway as a solution. Golfers have golf carts. Commuters have bikes. And for many, good old-fashioned walking is preferred.[14]

In order to build a loyal customer base for your startup, you must provide something uniquely and consistently valuable to them. Honestly assess how your offering is compelling or advantageous in the customer's eyes, whether through pilot projects, customer feedback, or, at a minimum, a thorough discussion and analysis of how your envisioned product will differentiate itself as experienced by the buying public.

All of these questions are intended to give you a taste of what it means to go beyond untested confidence in your idea and develop a more coherent understanding of market forces and opportunities related to your startup idea. For a more thorough set of questions, see the Market Readiness section of Appendix A. For all of these market questions, be sure to distinguish which of your answers are based on hopes or assumptions, versus verifiable facts, and find ways to test those.

CHAPTER FIVE

Your Math Story

Charting a Path to Breakeven and Beyond

"Numbers rule the Universe."

—Pythagoras

Remember the tale of Icarus and his passionate flight toward the sun? Although the story ended in tragedy, it began as an example of entrepreneurship at its best. Daedalus, the father, was the idea guy. He might have watched birds fly high above the prison walls for months before his *eureka* moment. He then devised a plan of escape and built wings of wax and feathers. When the time was right, he and Icarus launched themselves out over the sea, flapping their way to freedom. The exhilaration of that moment must have exceeded anything felt by passionate entrepreneurs before or since.

Underneath the courage and emotion, however, Icarus and Daedalus's flight was a product of basic physics. As an engineer, Daedalus was dealing with the interplay of opposing forces: the upward lift created by his wings versus the downward pull of gravity, and the forward push of those wings against the resistant drag of incoming wind. That flight was subject to the same set of physical laws that have governed every flight through the ages, whether by birds, planes, or winged mythological people.

In the same way, certain immutable laws of commerce will dictate whether or not your new venture makes it off the ground. You must convert your raw idea into something that will fly, a model that generates lift and minimizes drag, one that is fast and light enough to become airborne before the runway ends. Liftoff will prove that your model is sound, that it's aerodynamically suited to prevailing market conditions and financial realities, but it won't guarantee that your craft will stay aloft over time or arrive at a favorable destination. At times, your startup experience will feel like flying through dense fog while sitting in a cockpit full of mysterious buttons and levers.

The best way to cut through this early fog is to plan and manage your startup with the right level of rigor and realism. This means grasping the basic math underlying your business concept—how your approach will lead to near-term profits and longer-term value creation. Doing so will not only bring your immediate priorities into clear focus, but will help you accurately estimate how much starting capital you will need to reach breakeven and beyond.

As we saw in Chapter Two, entrepreneurial optimism can lead to rose-colored plans or no planning at all. Passion-trapped entrepreneurs tend to manage by assumption, believing that if they charge forward with enough commitment and hard work, all will be well with the numbers. Some are bored or intimidated by financial matters or have grown tired of spreadsheets that mask important issues instead of clarifying them. As a result, these founders lose touch with the sharp clarity offered by the bottom line and develop a kind of dysfunctional detachment from the economic factors that will make or break their business.

The solution is to balance your startup passion with *dispassionate* methods of planning and analysis. Passion and logic are complementary forces, and the most effective entrepreneurs bring extremely high levels of both. Returning to the metaphor of your new venture as an aircraft, passion is the jet fuel that accelerates it forward. Logic and its close cousins (i.e., good data, sound math, intellectual rigor, and critical thinking skills) provide the engineering, direction, and steering so that you can aim yourself in the right direction and adjust your progress as you go.

In the sections that follow, I'll address three areas of focus that will help you convert your idea and your passion into a business with tangible, enduring value:

1. *Planning.* What planning approach makes sense for your business, and what principles will help you make the most of your enthusiasm without getting trapped by it?

2. *Math.* What is your *math story,* the organizing logic of your venture, with numbers attached, and how will the elements of your business come together in a way that is profitable over time?

3. *Funding.* How will you bridge the gap between the amount of money your startup will need and what you currently have on hand?

Planning Is Clear Thinking

A common question among aspiring founders is whether to develop a full-blown business plan and, if so, what to include in it. According to most business schools and books on entrepreneurship, writing a business plan is one of the first essential tasks of launching a business. It's a rite of passage, one that has spawned its own support industry: business plan competitions, websites offering sample business plans (enter the search term "business plan" for a quick tour), and services that will write your business plan for you.

At the same time, we all know successful business owners who never bothered with a written plan, who just leapt in, and some studies that show little or no correlation between the writing of a business plan and startup success.[1] A number of experts insist that business planning is actually counterproductive to the startup process, because it siphons valuable time and attention away from more urgent tasks (such as selling), is full of assumptions and flat-out guesses about an unknowable future, and locks the business into a singular path when flexibility and agility are paramount.[2]

But the question of whether or not to plan represents a false choice. If you are thinking about your venture's future (and who isn't?), you are planning. Every founder anticipates future events, determines goals and objectives, weighs options, and decides how to proceed and what to do next—all basic planning activities. The real issue is one of effectiveness. So, ask yourself: *What kind of planning/thinking approach will best support the current needs of my business?*

MATCH YOUR PLANNING TO YOUR PHASE

Too often, planning approaches for mature organizations are unnecessarily applied to seed-stage businesses. The right approach for you will vary depending on where you are in your new venture life cycle. For this purpose, let's look at typical planning needs at three phases in a typical startup journey.

GESTATION/PRODUCT DEVELOPMENT – Here, you are incubating your startup idea, developing your product or service, learning about your market, and maybe gathering some early customer feedback. Your goal is to build something that meets a market need, one that customers will pay to have resolved. Your most important question is: *Do we have a concept that anyone (other than us) cares about?* In this phase, planning should focus on how to prove your concept, learn about potential markets, set priorities, and coordinate next steps. You can lay out a low-cost development path and identify key milestones, but some elements of a traditional business plan, such as extensive revenue projections, make little sense. If you don't yet have a compelling product or a workable business model, focus on developing these, instead of guessing how much money you will make. One of the common mistakes of early entrepreneurs, especially those in love with their idea, is behaving as if they have launched a stable business when, in fact, they are still in the cave of gestation.

CONSISTENT REVENUE – Once you have achieved some level of recurring sales, everything changes. Early revenue doesn't always translate into a profitable business, so your key question becomes: *Can we actually make money at this, and how?* Your sights now shift to the goal of breaking even, the point at which your venture can fund itself. Here is where the development of a clear, compelling *math story* is invaluable. The math story, to be outlined in the next section, answers questions such as: What is our business model, our competitive advantage, and our strategy? What is our path to breakeven (including pro forma profit and loss projections)? What are projected cash flows, and how will we manage our burn rate? What control mechanisms do we need in place to manage forward? How much capital will we need to reach profitability?

Whether or not you need a written business plan at this stage depends on your financing and communication needs. If you are seeking investors or lenders, you need a high-quality written plan, but be sure to learn what format your target investors require and what aspects of the plan they are most interested in. Even if you are not seeking funding, you may benefit from the discipline and rigor required to develop a business plan and find that it helps you communicate with stakeholders of all kinds. On the other hand, if you are working with only a handful of key team members, you can address the above questions and regularly review your key financial metrics without pulling together a formal plan. A decent-sized whiteboard and simplified financial snapshots will do just fine.

BEYOND BREAKEVEN/GROWTH – Once a business is self-funding, everything changes again. If you want to continue to grow, the operative questions are: *Is this business scalable? How can we create significant value over time?* Here, you will benefit from a disciplined planning approach that is widely communicated and regularly updated. Once you have found a robust market, scaling your business is all about executing. Identifying and coordinating resources, finding ways to grow efficiently, maintaining a hawk-like focus on key growth drivers, and understanding and mitigating risk factors are all critical to scaling a young business. In the growth phase, a well-managed planning process can be the difference between a healthy, thriving venture and one that overreaches, stalls, or flames out.

THREE VENTURES, THREE APPROACHES

In thinking about your approach to planning, consider the maturity of your venture. How fully developed is your product or service? Do you understand customer receptivity and demand? Do you know what will be required to successfully bring your offering to market? The underlying issue here is the relative number of knowns vs. unknowns: the more predictable your path forward, the more valuable a detailed, written business plan becomes. To illustrate, here are three quick examples:

DECISION ONE MORTGAGE – While he was incubating his startup idea as a senior leader at First Union, J.C. Faulkner knew that his new mortgage venture would target a well-known core need (i.e., home ownership) with well-established products in a rapidly growing market that he deeply understood. He had built successful mortgage shops and had been through many rounds of annual sales and cost projections. He knew the kind of people he would need and what he would pay them. He could accurately estimate an overall cost structure. In short, although he would encounter the unpredictable twists and turns all entrepreneurs do, he faced more knowns than unknowns. For all these reasons, he developed a thorough business plan with detailed financial projections over a three-year period to give himself a high-confidence roadmap for raising capital and growing the business.

MODALITY – At the time of his first round of funding, Mark Williams was dealing with uncertainty by the bucketful. He was still in a product development mode, having tested a raw concept with medical students and possessing what he hoped was a fairly mature prototype. He couldn't yet produce, sell, or deliver anything of substance. And his hypothetical customers swirled about in a poorly understood, just-emerging market. Even if he could identify the right users, he had no reliable distribution channel for delivery of the product (remember, this was pre-iPhone, pre-AppStore). And he still lacked the formal blessing of his most important partner, Apple Computer, as he patiently built relationships within the company in hopes that it would not crush him like a bug.

In the summer of 2006, Mark's attorneys developed a private placement memorandum (PPM), a standard fund-raising document outlining for prospective investors what Modality was all about. It included high-level information about the product idea, the assumed market need, existing licensing agreements, points of risk, and so forth. Only a single page in the eighty-page document dealt with financial forecasts, using a very simple chart with assumed prices, sales, costs, margins and some projected earnings per title figures. According to these projections, the company would produce and release 400 titles by the end of 2007, earning an annual average of $8,260 for each title. Total company profits were not included, but an investor could easily calculate Modality's rough projected earnings to exceed $3 million for 2007. Mark and his team knew that these projections were indeed rough. In fact they were guesses, based on little factual data and a raft of assumptions. As the PPM affirmed in understated fashion, "the forward-looking information provided in this Memorandum may prove inaccurate."

Because of the high levels of uncertainty at the time, Mark's planning approach was to continually sharpen priorities, in order to stay focused on a small set of mission-critical tasks. No formal business plan here. Just all hands on deck, pinching pennies, 24-7, with each month bringing a new make-or-break challenge. Everyone's effort and attention was on the very next task that would take Modality toward that landmark day when revenue would begin to flow.

THE IVEY – In Lynn Ivey's case, she and her financial modelers applied later-stage planning approaches and financial assumptions to an unproven, early-stage concept. Based on her first business plan, developed for investors in the spring of 2006, The Ivey seemed like a mature concept ready to go to market with a high degree of certainty. Lynn had a compelling and clear vision of her product, business model, and client base. She was confident that she could quickly fill up the facility with members. Her information packet for investors contained ten years of financial projections with annual revenues, cash flows, earnings, and rates of return.

The fact that her plan included the development of a high-value real estate asset in a preferred area of the city gave investors confidence, and it also drove her financial forecasting. She started with the total up-front cost of the building, added to it the overall cost structure required to operate a world-class service from it, and worked backward to create sales projections that would guarantee an acceptable path to profitability. Lynn's attitude at the time was, "Whatever it takes, we can do it."

But in reality, just like Mark Williams, Lynn was in the earliest stages of product development and gestation, facing many unknowns. In one sense, the most predictable aspect of her vision, the building, didn't matter. Her real product would not be the physical facility, but rather the services that would flow out of it, and, on this front, she had no factual evidence that her service concept was viable. She was trying something that had never been done before, and no amount of planning or projecting could accurately predict in advance how the service would play out in the real world. Looking back now, Lynn wishes she had invested more of her upfront money in more thoroughly investigating the market for an upscale adult daycare service, finding ways to test her concept before committing to millions of dollars of fixed costs. Depending on how her early experimentation went, she might have delayed construction in order to more fully prove her concept. She might also have been able to utilize her personal savings (she invested more than $400,000 into the company) in a low-cost pilot approach that may have gained enough traction to remove the need for outside investors. Or, at a minimum, this path would have helped her establish more realistic sales projections, based on actual market responsiveness instead of on a grand vision, and allowed her to plot a more steady, realistic path to profitability.

Constructing a Compelling Math Story

Your *math story* is the driving narrative of your business, defining what you are attempting to build and how, with numbers attached. A good math story cuts through the window dressing attached to most business plans and homes in on issues and variables that should be kept front-of-mind. It connects your story line with your bottom line, setting your intended trajectory and identifying the factors most likely to impact it. Your math story is also a mechanism for bringing the best of your passion, what you care most deeply about, together with planning and logic in the right measure.

During D1's explosive growth years, J.C. Faulkner often referred to his math story, which brought together the key elements of his vision, strategy, and business plan in a simple, coherent narrative. It served as a focusing mechanism and an anchor for every significant decision and action. "Even before launching, I spent a year fine-tuning my math story of what the new business would look like," he said. "It's like I did dress rehearsals for this new marriage for twelve months."

As an added benefit, J.C.'s math story helped him skillfully recruit key team members, investors, and other partners. "The one thing that created trust," he said, "was that people could see that I had a tremendous amount of confidence in what I was talking about. I had figured out the math story so well, and could explain it in such a logical fashion, people clearly understood why this business would be successful. The more they understood it, the more they wanted to be a part of it." Like many entrepreneurs, J.C. is naturally optimistic, but his deep confidence in D1 came from rigorous preparation and immersion in the right numbers, an area in which he thinks many fellow founders fall short. "Everybody wants their idea to work," he said. "And a lot of people try to sell their idea in vague terms, but they don't take the time to ground it, to operationalize it. The more you can make it granular to the point where it's irrefutable, or at least grounded in logic, the more people will get excited about it, both intellectually and emotionally."

Constructing a useful math story involves bringing together interlocking puzzle pieces from two sides of a single coin. The first side is your *core concept*, the organizing logic and rough shape of the business you want to create. Tim Berry, whose 2008 book *The Plan-As-You-Go Business Plan* I highly recommend, likens this conceptual core to the heart of an artichoke. It is the centerpiece around which all of your key decisions and week-to-week tactics are attached.[3] On the other side of the coin are *financial keys* that represent critical ratios or variables that will drive the early viability and health of your venture.

DEVELOP YOUR CORE CONCEPT

Good startup math rests on a business concept that makes sense for you and for the marketplace. Keeping it simple, you can think of your core concept as having three parts:

1. Your definition of success

2. Your strategy and business model

3. Your required capabilities and resources

These elements will be driven by, and grounded in, who you are as a founder (covered in Chapter Three) and the nature of your market opportunity (addressed in Chapter Four).

DEFINING SUCCESS – What's the point in knowing your numbers if they don't help you reach a compelling destination? Mountain climbers are fueled by an image of themselves on the summit, and successful founders are pulled toward an envisioned future that outperforms their current circumstances. *What future state would prompt you to give up what you have now and take on the risk and challenge of starting a business?*

An example of a fundamental choice you will face in defining success is how large a business you want to build and how you want to spend your time building it. J.C. Faulkner faced an early decision about D1's size that was driven mostly by his personal needs and goals. He launched the company with a five-person management team, incurring a significant expense that meant the new business would have to generate $8 million per month in loan volume to break even and would require $700,000 in upfront capital to become profitable. Alternatively, he estimated that he could start with a two-person management team, break even at $3 million in monthly volume, and spend only $300,000 to get there. "The reason I didn't choose that route," he said, "is because I didn't want to be on a two-person management team and have to live that way. I would have been doing twice as much work once we were up and running. I knew I would enjoy working with a bigger team a lot more, and I would be able to spend a lot more time with my family." What many would see as a greater risk, spending $700,000 in upfront capital instead of $300,000, J.C. actually saw as lower risk, because it better aligned with his personal goals and allowed him to tap into a wider base of management talent. The larger team would have the capacity to create a much larger company, which also aligned with his longer-term definition of success.

CONCEIVING YOUR STRATEGY AND BUSINESS MODEL – Your strategy defines what business you are in: what you provide, for whom, and why. Your business model dictates how you will configure the pieces of your business system together as a profitable whole. Hundreds of books have been written on the topic of business models and strategy, and experts will forever quibble and wordsmith around the edges of these concepts. But the core of your business blueprint will most often be driven by the following questions:

- *What products or services will you offer? To what customers or markets?*

- *What is your value premise and how will you deliver it?*

- *How will you acquire customers and distribute your product or service to them?*

- *What price will the market bear? Will this generate a healthy profit for you?*

- *What will set your business apart from the rest? How will you overtake and defend against competitive forces?*

- *What factors will make or break your model? In what areas must you excel in order for your model to succeed?*

- *How will you experiment, learn, and continually reformulate your model as you go forward?*

Many of the answers to these questions will reveal themselves over time as you execute on your game plan, but it's vital to think about them early and deeply. One of the refreshing advantages of being a startup, relative to established competitors, is that you possess the power of a blank sheet of paper, the ability to shape your path forward without being shackled by existing commitments, partnerships, infrastructure, or inventory. Big companies are battleships; you are the speedboat, still at dock. Spend time clarifying your intentions. Lay down a rough outline of your future business. What will your business look like after it is up and running? Will it be large or small? Selling products or services? Mass market or niche player? Consumer-focused or B2B? Known for blazing speed, high quality, or low price?

Mark Kahn's idea for his second startup, TRAFFIQ, was to create a platform directly connecting buyers and sellers of online ads—to become the eBay of Web advertising. The value proposition was clear—he was not the first or the last to envision an online advertising marketplace. He believed two factors would make or break his venture. The first was building a high-performance, high-capacity technology platform. The second would be his ability to scale: to attract and serve a large number of buyers and sellers in an ever-increasing, self-reinforcing loop of success. The value of the marketplace would be directly proportional to the number and quality of its users. Using the eBay example, Mark explains, "On eBay, if a buyer is looking for children's toys and I've got a lot of sellers who are selling presidential pins, that's no good. The market is not providing value. So it's about making matches. And if TRAFFIQ makes matches, then it provides liquidity, and if it provides liquidity, it builds scale; and if you can build scale, you make it defensible."

Similar to TRAFFIQ, Mark Williams positioned Modality as a conduit between buyers and sellers. On one side were the traditional print publishers, who owned large vaults of branded educational content. On the other were iPod-toting students, who wanted digital versions of educational titles on their mobile devices. Modality's approach was to lock up rights to publisher content in the form of licensing agreements and move as quickly as possible to convert and sell this content to iPod users. Because of the free-wheeling, Wild West nature of the AppStore distribution channel, a make-or-break factor for Modality would be its ability to transition from a wide array of early products—in effect, a kind of experimental spaghetti-against-the-wall approach—to more focused investment in bestselling product categories. In the market fog of nearly 100,000 competitive titles being sold in the same channel, gaining and analyzing relevant sales data would prove as difficult as it was vital.

Although every venture will face its own unique set of challenges and opportunities, strong strategies tend to have a few common threads. First, a good strategy meets the challenge of customer acquisition head on. How are you going to find customers, and how will you guarantee sales success? I can't think of anything more vital to a young business. Second, strategy is about focus, which means saying "no." Don't fall into the habit of picking up every shiny object that appears along your path. Third, strategy drives, and is driven by, your core identity. What is unique, unchangeable, non-negotiable, or indestructible about your business? What makes you *you*, and how does this translate into a competitive advantage?

ESTIMATING CAPABILITIES AND RESOURCES – Once you have envisioned how you will create and deliver your offering, you can broadly estimate what capabilities, tools, systems, and other resources will be required to set up and run the business. *What will it take to launch your business model? What basic building blocks will form the foundation of your overall cost structure?* This step is partly creative, like crafting and assembling the pieces of a puzzle, and partly analytic, starting with broad categories like talent, technology, or capital equipment, then breaking those down into component parts. Your ability to accurately estimate these requirements will depend on your business stage, the maturity of your concept, your understanding of the market, and so on. But be sure to sketch out, as clearly as you can, what will be needed along what timelines to put your business model in place and get your venture up and running.

As you think about how to bring your business model to life, push yourself to understand and utilize the more innovative options available to you. Today's entrepreneur can benefit from a mind-boggling array of tools and systems to get things done, access customers, and deliver offerings. You can build a global brand from your basement and distribute new products across the world with the click of a mouse. An example is the game-changing practice of *crowdsourcing*, popularized by Jeff Howe's book of the same name, allowing you to build and test sophisticated products at unprecedented speed and minimal cost.[4]

KNOW YOUR FINANCIAL KEYS

Intimately tied to your core concept is a set of financial keys that reflect the trajectory and health of your venture. Most founders don't possess financial modeling skills, and detailed financials won't be necessary for all businesses. But every founder can work to understand the right numbers and ensure that the necessary calculations are done, even if these are sketched out on a legal pad or the back of an envelope. Entrepreneur Bob Reiss, in his book *Low Risk, High Reward*, calls this ability "numeracy," the numbers equivalent of literacy, and likens it to understanding a second language. "Numeracy is a way of thinking," he writes. "Thinking in numbers is a vital, vital skill."[5] If your financial projections do require complex calculations, partner with a talented finance pro who can help you conduct analyses at the right level of rigor and detail.

The first purpose of these financial keys is to determine whether your core concept is economically viable so you can avoid pouring your time and your passion into a money-losing business model. Just as important, understanding and focusing on the right numbers allows you to monitor and improve your concept as you go. It gives you a reliable instrument panel as you fly through the early startup fog.

Depending on the size, stage, and complexity of your venture, you will need to develop a system of financial forecasting and tracking that works for you. Regardless of the type of business you are launching, however, the following financial keys will provide a solid foundation for growing a healthy venture:

- Understanding profitability dynamics
- Building pro forma financial projections
- Mastering cash flow

UNDERSTANDING THE PROFITABILITY DYNAMICS – Grasping the factors that will drive profit within your particular business model is the starting point for building a compelling math story. Investors and owners use several common metrics to think about profitability and returns, including return on invested capital (ROIC), return on assets (ROA), and return on equity (ROE). Tools for calculating these measures can be found in any startup finance book or on countless websites. The differences between these measures are less significant than the common question they pose: *What is your venture's return on the resources and assets that you (and possibly others) have put into it?*

Keeping it simple, the fundamental truth related to your startup's profitability and prospects for growth is reflected in a universal formula, popularized many years ago by Ram Charan and Noel Tichy in their book *Every Business Is a Growth Business.*[6] The formula can be applied to any business, large or small, simple or complex. Charan and Tichy make the point that successful street vendors, as well as CEOs, understand its truth, and I have found it to be a powerful tool in helping new founders cut through financial complexity and get to the heart of profitability. It is:

$$R = M \times V$$

where *R* stands for return, *M* refers to profit margin (what is left over after expenses have been subtracted from sales), and *V* refers to velocity (the rate at which your total asset base creates revenue). In the airline business, the profit from each flight represents margin, whereas the number of flights that can be squeezed into a given time period represents velocity. In a consulting business, each billable consulting day generates a fee with a built-in profit margin. Velocity measures how many consulting days are sold and delivered per consultant.

Think about dinner at your favorite restaurant. The owner wants to maximize her "return on dinner." Her basic profit margin (*M*) will be a function of the average dinner ticket per customer (how much each customer orders and at what prices) minus the average cost of serving each customer (total costs divided by total number of customers). Great restaurant managers are continually looking for ways to increase margins. They can raise prices, squeeze out costs, or steer customers toward higher margin dishes. Velocity (*V*), in this example, is represented by how many guests can be served during a single dinner period. To increase velocity, the owner can turn tables more quickly with reservation schedules that accommodate three seatings

per night, or the owner can streamline the processes for seating customers, serving them, and taking their payments. The more customers
she can serve in a given space and time, the greater the velocity and,
therefore, the greater her "return on dinner."

Any founder can use $R = M \times V$ as a framework for thinking about
how to increase profits and grow his or her business. *How can you utilize
these two big levers for making money? How can you improve your margins?
Do you have any upward flexibility on price? Can you reduce your cost of sales,
your cost of delivery, or your fixed cost base? How can you increase your velocity?
How do you increase sales volume? Generate repeat purchases? Deliver your
product or service more efficiently to clear the way for new sales? How can you
"turn your tables" more quickly?*

Note that margin and velocity are both tied to market realities.
They both depend on the fit between your offering and customer demand for it. The price your customers will pay for your offering is a
function of how well you are solving a core problem for them. And
the world's greatest strategy for quickly turning tables won't matter if
enough customers don't show up.

Also, nearly every entrepreneur encounters tradeoffs between
margin and velocity. Actions taken to increase your margins can lead
to reductions in sales volume. Alternatively, pumping up sales might
call for tactics that cut into profits. The key is to understand how the
two factors interact *within your particular business model*, and use this
knowledge to optimize the relationship and any tradeoffs between the
two.

BUILDING PRO FORMA FINANCIAL PROJECTIONS – At the heart of your
math story are projections that trace the expected economic path of
your startup over a specified future period. *Pro forma* is Latin for "according to form," and these forecasts lay out your trajectory if all goes
as planned. In addition to a standard profit and loss (P&L) pro forma,
showing expected revenues, expenses, and bottom line results over
the first few years, you also want to do cash flow and balance sheet
projections. For prospective investors and bankers, you typically need
to provide monthly projections for year one and annual projections
through at least three years.

Most venture founders develop detailed forecasts on interactive spreadsheets, often with the help of a skilled financial analyst, but, in some cases, simpler tools will do. Many years ago, when I was building my first solo consulting practice, I sat down at the beginning of each year with several blank sheets of paper. I sketched out expected revenues for the coming year per client and client category, noting any anticipated changes to my operating budget and when those expenses would occur. Using these pages, I could easily anticipate cash flows, based on knowledge of client payment schedules and vendor costs, and determine where and how to direct any business development efforts. This pencil-and-paper system worked fine for me, because my business model was simple. Margins were high, and revenues, expenses, and cash flows were easy to track. This system allowed me to sketch "what if" scenarios and explore the effect of hypothetical changes in my client base, my fee structure, and so on.

As with all attempts to predict the future, your pro forma will be a guess. For some founders, it's a highly informed, educated guess. For others, it's a pie-in-the-sky dream. Either way, it's likely to be wrong. So, beyond the obvious reason that investors or bankers might require them, why go to the trouble of building detailed financial projections?

First, building your pro forma is an exercise in logic that helps you pinpoint those variables most critical to your success. I once worked with the founder of a pre-revenue startup who obsessed over finding the cheapest possible outsourced vendor to create his first technology product. He had resisted running financial projections on his startup idea, but my partner and I insisted. Once projections were available, he easily saw how outsourcing costs were virtually nothing compared to his guaranteed salary and that of his co-founders. His focus quickly shifted to the question of how to radically reduce salary payments until a few projects could generate reliable revenue.

Second, the pro forma is a soft tablet through which vital connections between the critical elements of your business story can be understood. Your first pro forma statement will be an unanimated snapshot of the future, but with the help of a skilled analyst, you can run sensitivity analyses between key variables, playing out various "what if" scenarios. What happens if we launch more aggressively than planned, doubling our staff and doubling our sales? How would this affect cash flows? Or what if we launch much more conservatively, bootstrapping our way to growth? What kind of capital would each scenario require and at what times? In this way, you can spot potential trouble spots, as well as unexpected windows of opportunity, far enough in advance to do something about them.

To guard against the common tendency toward overly optimistic projections, you will be wise to run best-, mid-, and worst-case scenarios for your sales and expense projections. Lynn Ivey encountered three major negative forces as she attempted to get The Ivey up and running: a grand opening that occurred six months later than projected, a first year of sales that fell more than 90 percent below projections, and a steep recession that started a year after she launched. She never seriously factored these scenarios into her planning, and instead relied on a single, optimistic view of the future. When these events unfolded, she had no strong contingency plan.

Third, your pro forma will train your eye on the path to profitability and key milestones along the way. One of these is the highly anticipated day that you break even, the day you begin to generate cash instead of burn it. Whether it's projected to be in your third month or your third year, your breakeven point has a kind of catalyzing pull to it. Like a visible hilltop, it's a milestone that you and your team will strive to reach.

Finally, your pro forma projections will help you estimate how much capital will be needed to get your business safely off the ground. You can anticipate cash needs or crises and prepare for them in advance. By the time Lynn Ivey's money became dangerously thin, her initial funding sources were tapped out, and she had to scramble to raise funds from a position of weakness rather than strength.

MASTERING CASH FLOW – Cash is like oxygen for a new venture, so mastering cash flow is a pivotal challenge for all entrepreneurs. Joel Kurtzman, through his extensive research underlying the book *Startups That Work*, identified positive cash flow as one of a handful of critical success factors for venture success and a key driver of longer-term value creation.[7]

As any seasoned business owner or investor can attest, profitability doesn't guarantee healthy cash flow. Cash is a product of payment timing, forward-looking investments, billing and collections practices, and other variables that, taken together, can have a counterintuitive effect on cash levels. One of the ironies of early venture success is that rapid growth can cause uninvited cash flow crises to arrive with little or no warning.

I am not ready to jump on the trendy bandwagon of pundits proclaiming bootstrapping, launching your business at minimal expense and with scant starting capital, as the only credible way to build a business. As I'll outline in the next section on funding, I believe that startup founders who afford themselves a healthy financial cushion, in whatever form, enjoy a higher likelihood of success than the typical entrepreneur. But even the most well-financed entrepreneur can operate with a bootstrapper's mindset to ensure healthy cash generation and management.

Beyond the usual focus on prudent spending practices, I recommend the following keys to managing your cash.

First, *stay on top of your cash situation*. Make this a non-negotiable management practice. Review your cash levels, cash flows, burn rate, and budget vs. actual expenses on a frequent, regular basis, at least weekly early in your launch. Bob Reiss advocates for the creation and review of a weekly financial snapshot, or "flash report,"[8] and most highly successful businesspeople I know sit down on a regular basis to conduct such a review. For some, it's Saturday morning coffee with their finance person. For others, it's a routine weekday meeting. It sounds boring, and it sometimes is, but skip this practice at your peril.

Second, *look far ahead down cash-flow road*. The definition for "far" will vary depending on your type of business and your situation, but once you realize that you have only a few months of cash left, it's often too late to do anything about it. Raising money often takes four to six months in the best of circumstances, and major expense cuts can take several months to have a positive impact on cash flow.

Third, *don't delegate your ultimate accountability for the numbers*. Many startup founders wisely outsource bookkeeping and financial analysis tasks. Eventually, with growth, you'll need a trusted controller and/or

CFO in-house to stay on top of the numbers and conduct forward-looking analyses. But you should always be plugged in to what's happening with your financial keys. When it comes to early stage financials, you are the worrier-in-chief. Don't count on anyone else to be lying awake at three in the morning, deciding where to trim costs or find additional capital.

Securing the Right Funding

One of the benefits of developing a clear math story and accurately anticipating future cash flows is getting a clear picture of your venture's capital requirements. In his classic book, *Growing a Business*, Paul Hawken quotes Abraham Lincoln in making a point about funding. "How long should a man's legs be?" Lincoln said, "Long enough to reach the ground." How much money does your startup need? In Hawken's view, you need enough money to "get to market."[9]

But exactly how much money this means is not always clear, and an intense debate has risen over the past decade about the value and wisdom of raising any startup capital at all. On one side is the well-worn bootstrapper's path, full of proud, gritty, ramen-eating stalwarts, who disdain any form of outside capital. Some proponents of this view believe that early money in the bank causes founding teams to become lazy, to become unfocused and undisciplined, and to lose touch with the market realities. Others cite the importance of retaining maximum control over the venture and one's equity stake in it, as well as avoiding the risky burden of debt.

On the other side are investors and entrepreneurs who advocate for well-capitalized ventures, pointing to evidence that better-funded businesses succeed at higher rates.[10] Over the years, I've heard several founders who take this view say, "I'd rather own a small slice of a something very successful than a major piece of something that fails." Based on my experience and research, I take this view as well, believing that your level of passion and preparation, as well as the market demand for your concept, are independent of how you capitalize your business. If you are capable, committed, and prepared as a founder; if you bring a healthy market orientation and have identified real market demand for your idea; and if you have planned with rigor and realism and have worked out a compelling math story, why wouldn't you do what it takes to fully fund your plan's success?

I do observe, on a regular basis, the dangers of unchecked spending. But spending too much money, per se, is never the real cause of new venture failure. The cause is spending it on the wrong things, which typically means overspending in some areas and underspending in others. Lynn Ivey now regrets not putting more money into upfront market development and proving that her high-end concept would fly, and she would avoid pouring upfront funds into a fixed real estate asset.

Here is a set of principles to help you think about funding your venture, whether that funding comes from personal savings or outside sources:

- *Take the long view.* Work to understand the longer-term implications of your funding decisions. Too many entrepreneurs solve today's problems in ways that limit future options. For example, raising your initial money by getting small donations from a large group of friends and family members may be the easiest approach in the short run, but you may regret it later, as more sophisticated later-stage funders often avoid deals with large groups of investors attached.

- *Understand your control needs.* Few funding sources come without some loss of control. Are you willing to cede total control and build your venture under some form of investor or lender oversight?

- *Dig the well before you are thirsty.* Raise money before you need it. Nothing scares away investors and lenders like an entrepreneur in financial crisis. If you have developed a clear math story, you should be able to anticipate where critical investments will be needed to get your business off the ground. Because raising capital usually takes longer than expected, wise founders are always thinking about future sources of funds and cultivating those sources.

- *Raise more money than you think you will need.* New owners typically view their business through rose-colored glasses, overestimating early revenues and underestimating early costs. A general rule of thumb: Determine what you will need for a successful launch, in realistic terms, and then double it. Everything will take longer, and cost more, than you expect.

- *Realize that raising money does not equate to spending it.* You can manage your business with a bootstrapper's mindset while maintaining access to a healthy reserve. Invest with confidence in areas of clear priority, but stay mindful of your overall expense base.

- *Consider a wide a spectrum of potential sources.* Consider personal savings, financing from banks, equity investments or personal loans from friends/family, angel or venture capital investors, bootstrapping, etc., but understand the tradeoffs associated with each.

- *Understand that funding choices are highly personal.* Your decisions about funding your business will be driven by your purpose, desired lifestyle, risk-tolerance, etc. There is no single "right" approach to funding your business.

CHAPTER SIX

Startup Agility
Executing with Focused Flexibility

"A startup is an experiment: An inquiry into how the world might look under the vision of the startup's founders."

—Eric Ries, Co-Founder, IMVU

Despite the eagerness and optimism of passionate entrepreneurs, there is no such thing as a sure thing. Each new venture is a learning lab in which the founder's ambitions and ideas are tested against market realities and cold financial facts. The birth of a business is an inherently creative process in which possibilities are generated, torn apart, refined, and reconstituted, all to adapt to environmental uncertainty that will persist long after the startup phase.

Passionate founders must especially guard against betting the bulk of their resources onto a singular, unforgiving strategy. As we move into the second decade of the twenty-first century, commercial markets are increasingly turbulent due to the transformational effect of technology on all facets of business and life, redefining how products and services are designed, produced, purchased, delivered, and serviced.[1] Amid this uncertainty, executing with agility is more vital than ever.

In 2006 and 2007, Mark Williams and his team poured their time, energy, and capital into building out a range of learning products for Apple's click-wheel iPod, creating digital versions of well-known titles, such as *Netter's Anatomy* for medical students, *Frommer's Travel Guides* for vacationers, and *BrainQuest* digital flash cards for kids. The click-wheel device would soon seem as ancient as the rotary phone, but in 2007 it remained one of the hottest mobile devices on the planet.

As 2007 drew to a close, Modality's early product sales were sluggish—not nearly enough to cover its monthly burn rate—but Mark and his team remained optimistic because of advances in several areas. The iPod's internal architecture was virtually closed to third-party developers, so Modality built software that would write content directly to hidden database files on users' devices. Although technical barriers prevented Modality from selling products through Apple's iTunes platform, it created a web portal to allow iPod owners to directly buy and install the company's products. And, in a move that symbolized its growing support, Apple provided a spot in its popular retail stores for a test run of Modality's *BrainQuest* learning products.

Thanks to the team's passion and tenacity, Modality was beginning to gain momentum. It had finally figured out how to sell and distribute early products, and relationships with Apple and publishing partners were improving week by week. Mark Williams looked toward 2008 as the year when his team's innovation and persistence would pay off.

But in January of 2008, he learned that paradigm-rattling changes were on the way. After years of closely guarding the operational guts of its devices, Apple was preparing to open up the iPhone to software developers around the world. The company planned to release a Software Development Kit (SDK) in March, hoping to spark a flood of innovative iPhone applications from both professional and amateur programmers. Mark had kept an eye on the iPhone since its release six months earlier, thinking it would be the next logical device for his products. But Apple's 180-degree shift from super secrecy to wide-open invitation caught nearly everyone by surprise.

Apple's turnabout presented a painful choice for Mark and his team. Switching their full focus to the new iPhone would mean stalling, and ultimately abandoning, their hard-won progress on the click-wheel frontier. But staying with the click-wheel iPod would leave them as undisputed masters of a once-great but forgotten technology. Mark decided to give up his "bird in the hand" in hopes of seizing what new opportunities might lay in the bush.

The next few months were a whirlwind of innovation, salesmanship, and surprise for him: Trips to Cupertino, California, to share his iPhone-based prototype with Apple; word from Apple that Steve Jobs loved the prototype; and then an invitation to join Jobs on stage at Apple's World Wide Developer Conference (WWDC) in June. The June 2008 WWDC functioned as a coming-out party for the AppStore distribution channel and for the new generation iPhone. When called upon, Mark took the stage and made the most of his twenty minutes, walking the audience through a demo of the Modality *Netter's Anatomy* application that featured high-definition, colorful, zoomable screen shots of human heart, brain, nerve, and bone anatomy. Apple's online AppStore, the channel that would forever change the face of mobile computing, would soon make its debut, featuring Modality's first iPhone-based *Netter's Anatomy* digital flash cards priced at $39.99.

Mark had bet big on the iPhone and the AppStore, and he needed a significant revenue payoff to make it worthwhile. "If we don't get a good bump from this," he said at the time, "we might need to talk about how to close this thing down." Fortunately, by mid-August, sales had gone through the roof: five *Netter's Anatomy* titles alone had grossed more than $600,000 for the month of July. For the time being, Modality had survived a dangerous blow, and had positioned itself as a force to be reckoned with in the emerging mobile learning space.

Mark Williams's story illustrates a common experience for entrepreneurs, who must often let go of cherished strategies or hard-earned assets in order to seize new opportunities and deal with emerging threats. With the benefit of hindsight, Mark's decision to aggressively redirect his resources into iPhone development seems like an obvious move, a no-brainer. But at the time, it meant trading away a newly stable platform for a disrupting dose of uncertainty. It required a psychological openness to change and a high degree of operational agility, attributes that would continue to be vital as Modality's operation grew in size and complexity. The broader lesson here is that highly successful ventures almost always diverge from the founder's original intentions, a fact that places a premium on openness, learning, and agility.

In this chapter I'll outline two core attributes that drive strong and agile execution. The first is an ability to manage the paradoxical tension between whole-hearted commitment and wide-eyed flexibility. The second is developing a healthy approach to iteration, meaning that you rapidly iterate your business idea, capture lessons learned, and capitalize on your learning by making smart, tough calls about how to change your product, your business model, or, in certain cases, your venture's core identity.

The Paradox of Strong Execution

Chapters Three, Four, and Five each dealt with one of the fundamental domains that form the strong core of any new venture:

- Chapter Three addressed the principle of *founder readiness,* how to best prepare yourself and your team for the startup challenge.

- Chapter Four focused on the importance of developing a *market orientation,* understanding the customer problem you are solving and allowing your venture to be shaped from the outside-in.

- Chapter Five emphasized the value of a compelling *math story,* your organizing logic, your money-making formula, and your path to breakeven and beyond.

These three domains are the core components of your startup blueprint—the more skillfully and fully you address these components and the questions and issues that fall within them, the more promising your venture's odds of success. Shortcuts or compromises in these areas can leave your new business vulnerable to the downside risk of overheated passion or misdirected enthusiasm. But as fundamental and important as these domains are, your venture is going nowhere without skillful emphasis in a fourth domain, that of *effective execution.*

Figure 6-1 illustrates the four-quadrant framework for new venture success that my consulting partners and I use to assess and improve new venture performance. It highlights four core factors that differentiate successful growth ventures from those that stall or fail. In a perfect world, issues associated with the first three quadrants—the *founder,* the *market,* and the *math*—would be clearly understood and predictable, in which case strong execution would simply require the flawless implementation of a rock-solid, well-conceived plan. But in the real world, things are never so simple. All four domains are in constant motion, driven by external events, internal learning, and interdependence with each other. The cycling arrows within the model represent the always-iterating, ever-shifting nature of the startup journey.

Figure 6-1. Four-quadrant framework for new venture success.

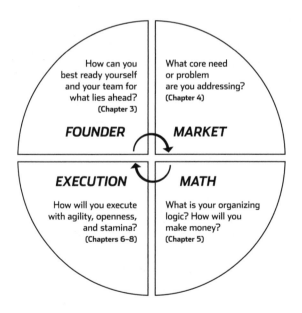

COMMITTING WITHOUT ATTACHING

In order to execute with agility, founders must successfully deal with a paradox. Effective entrepreneurs are able to completely commit to an idea, while remaining open to changing it. This ability to commit to a path without becoming attached to it is no simple skill. In athletics, the most agile athletes operate from a base of readiness, always under control, reading the field around them and quickly responding to teammates and competitors. They come with a game plan but quickly improvise if needed to respond to unfolding events. They skillfully manage the tension between rehearsed and spontaneous movement.

A similar tension permeates every startup journey. By following your early plans, creating your first products and winning your first customers, you create a base of strength and a platform from which to move forward. But both successes and failures bring unforeseen opportunities and threats. You will need to reconsider early decisions and most likely shift your offerings and your model. This ongoing tension between your pride in what you have built and your unending desire to improve it is inherent in the process of bringing a concept to life. It is the nature of an evolving, iterating idea becoming real.

The greater our passion, the more likely it is that we will fall victim to cognitive biases that encourage us to stick with an early idea, even in the face of contradictory signals. The cognitive bias of *anchoring,* for example, leads us to give too much weight to our first big idea or strategy. We unconsciously filter new information so that it fits within our established view of the venture, instead of provoking us to see it in entirely new ways. Also coming into play is the *sunk cost fallacy,* the cognitive bias that pressures founders and investors to stick with an existing plan to avoid wasting previously invested time, money, and effort. The real mistake, however, comes in thinking that prior investments somehow justify the continuation of a losing strategy.

The ability to commit without attaching has benefits ranging far beyond the world of startups. Donald Sull, professor of management practice at the London Business School and a global expert on managing in turbulent markets, advises companies to "keep the vision fuzzy and the priorities clear," emphasizing the value of laser-like focus and crisp execution in the short term, while recognizing that longer-term events are ultimately unpredictable. "A fuzzy vision works," he writes, "because it provides general direction and sets aspirations without prematurely locking the company in to a specific course of action."[2]

Describing his approach to the same challenge, J.C. Faulkner uses the term *perch management*, evoking the example of a bird flying through a forest with a clear focus on the next landing place. Each leg of your startup journey will lead to a new "perch," from which a new vista opens up and another destination is chosen. "Long-range planning is important, but it's always wonderfully imperfect," he says. "So you should focus on what it takes to get to the next perch, to execute on your next logical step."

LOOKING THROUGH THE LENS OF POTENTIAL: LESSONS FROM A VISUAL ARTIST

Launching a new venture is a creative act, and challenges faced by passionate entrepreneurs run parallel in many ways to the work of professional artists. Like entrepreneurs, artists give shape and life to new ideas through processes of experimentation and discovery. And like most entrepreneurs, artists invest a great deal of passion and emotion in their work. Entrepreneurs can learn much from an accomplished artist, someone who has grounded a career in the creative process and who teaches creativity and innovation to business leaders.

I first met Shaun Cassidy as part of an entrepreneurial session at the Innovation Institute, a program in Charlotte, North Carolina, that brings professional artists together with senior executives to help them unleash personal creativity and build more innovative workplaces.[3] Shaun is an artist leader with the Institute, a professor of sculpture at Winthrop University, and an internationally recognized sculptor and painter. Much of his teaching centers on the theme that creativity is an iterative process, where one idea leads to the next, with each iteration building on a prior result toward an increasingly valuable piece of work. His creative process echoes my own founding experience and that of many successful entrepreneurs I have observed and studied.

Shaun tells the story of how his idea for an acclaimed public work started with a mistake. Working on a commissioned sculpture for a beer company during an art residency program in New York in 2005, he spilled wet concrete on an old sweater that had been a gift from his wife. In an effort to save the sweater, he let the concrete dry. "The next morning," he says, "I pulled the concrete out and found that the fibers from the woolen sweater had become embedded in the concrete." He set aside the concrete chunk for a day or two, and "began to recognize that this chance happening revealed a really interesting potential. And the potential was that if you cast concrete over woolen objects or fabrics, a residue of the fabric is going to get embedded into the concrete." This led him to an entire series of works where he cast concrete over woolen gloves, hats, and socks, then pulled the objects out, leaving a negative space in the concrete along with fibers from the clothing.

A year later, Shaun was awarded a commission to do a major public art project, a sculpture in a Charlotte park. The city sponsors wanted something highly durable and vandal proof to be built on a low budget. He and his assistant went around the community collecting clothing from the people who lived around the park. They then cast a long winding bench out of concrete, into which they embedded and removed the community members' clothing, leaving overlapping impressions of the community's personal belongings in the bench as it stretched through the park.

"The idea for that project," Shaun says, "could never have come had I not recognized the potential in that first mistake. And, to me, it is an example of how one thing can lead to another, and to another. If you trust the process and you let the process play out long enough—sometimes over years—your solutions to problems will be more innovative because you've got a richer pool from which to draw. If someone had sat me down and said, 'Well, design me a public art project,' and I hadn't had that experience in New York, I don't think that the solution would have been nearly as interesting."

Of the many lessons from Shaun Cassidy's work and teaching, here are some that are especially relevant for new venture founders:

- *Allow solutions to come through a process.* Shaun says that his conceiving is always the result of an iterative process. "It's never just sitting down and thinking of a good idea or coming up with a way to solve a problem. It's always the result of a process that might begin with something weird or accidental but then builds and improves over time."

- *Look through the lens of potential instead of rejection.* Shaun works with leaders to help them "develop a lens that will allow them to see the potential in almost anything instead of rejecting it instantly." Every iteration of an idea, he says, "contains a nugget of potential that can lead you to another iteration of the idea. So in that sense, nothing you do is ever wasted."

- *Don't settle too soon.* Shaun believes that too many people are content with early ideas, rather than pushing themselves to higher standards. "I think people settle way too soon," he says. "They're hell bent on coming up with the answer right now, instead of allowing it to develop and reveal itself. So, this idea of 'not settling' is very important to me. If you become static, you're lost."

- *Push for improvement until the very end.* Early in his career, just before graduate school in England, Shaun worked for Sir Anthony Caro, a legendary abstract sculptor, who would sometimes force radical changes at the last possible moment. "He would force us to weld these big sculptures. They would take six months, sometimes, and we would think we were closing in and finished. And if he thought there was a 1 percent chance that we could make these sculptures better, he would have us drag out the torch and cut these things in half, and flip them upside down. He would force us to make incredibly radical moves very, very late in the process. So this notion of laying it on the line *all the way through* the process, not just the beginning and the middle, but even at the end, in order to make something innovative and breathtaking, that was a real education."

- *Use disruption as a positive force.* One of Shaun's many artistic residencies was with the Djerassi Resident Artists Program in California. "In my own studio I have a lot of equipment welders, overhead crane, all this kind of stuff," he says. "I got to California and the director led me into the studio where I would be working. There was absolutely nothing in the studio, just polished concrete floor. Of all the residencies I have been on, that was the most disruptive to my normal creative habit. I had to spend the first week of that residency walking and thinking and reflecting upon what I wanted to do and responding to the emotional and physical characteristics of the site. I went to the hardware store with the facility guy's truck and bought a whole lot of wood, and bought a chop saw, and bought a cordless drill, and built this huge installation out in the landscape. And it never would have occurred to me to do that had I not been so disrupted from my normal flow. I think that I learned more about myself on that residency, and made probably the best work of my life because of that disruption."

As both Modality's change of direction and Shaun Cassidy's creative lessons illustrate, we can't fully predict what opportunities will emerge as our ideas become real. Therefore, the ability to read and adapt along the ever-changing startup road is vital to early-phase survival and longer-term growth. And although agility is essential, it is not enough. Equally crucial is our ability to learn—to shine a light through the fog of startup uncertainty and gather the relevant lessons to be found there.

The New Venture Learning Curve

Most founders look back on their startup journey as the most intensive educational experience of their lives. Even serial entrepreneurs, full of war stories, are amazed at what can be learned with each new venture. Rather than thinking of learning as a bonus, something to be gained while chasing customers and revenue, wise founders view learning as a *primary objective* of their startup launch. They are insatiable students of successes and failures, large and small. They dig for cause-and-effect relationships and erase uncertainty wherever possible. This mindset of discovery ensures that positive results are evaluated and put in perspective, and that the inevitable mistakes and misadventures bring value to the venture as well. Learning cannot be separated from your startup's performance because it *drives* startup performance.

Three practices will help you avoid a certainty-driven approach and, instead, launch your venture as a flexible process of discovery. The first is rapid, healthy iteration, a process that will drive and enrich your new venture learning curve. The second is to ensure that your cycles of iteration are occurring at multiple levels, beyond simply cranking out new product features. And the third is to capture relevant lessons in a balanced and holistic way, utilizing the four-quadrant model for new venture success.

HEALTHY ITERATION DRIVES LEARNING

Eric Ries, a software engineer and entrepreneur who launched his *Lessons Learned* blog in 2008 and quickly became a leading champion of "lean startup" principles for dealing with the pervasive uncertainty faced by new ventures, often opens his startup workshops with a pair of absurd videos.[4] The first features a confident Ali G (one of comedian Sacha Baron Cohen's fictional alter egos) pitching a product idea called the "Ice Cream Glove" to investors, including Donald Trump and a series of unwitting venture capital pros. The Ice Cream Glove is a rubber glove that Ali G claims will take the world by storm, because it allows people to eat ice cream cones without getting ice cream on their hands. Later in the video, he unveils his "hoverboard," basically a skateboard without wheels, which he hopes will be converted, thanks to venture capital funding, into a flying platform. These ideas are so comical that the most priceless aspects of the footage are Ali G's sincerity in pitching his concepts and the dumbfounded looks on his listeners' faces.

Ries's second video is an infomercial for the Snuggie, the "blanket with sleeves" that served as the butt of many jokes in late 2008 and 2009. The Snuggie-clad characters in the ad are hard to watch without guffawing, which is why so many first-time viewers of the ad thought it was a fictional spoof. But the Snuggie was no joke from a revenue and marketing standpoint. It sold more than 4 million units in its first few months and caught fire as a pop culture phenomenon, leading *USA Today* to proclaim in January of 2009, "The Cult of Snuggie threatens to take over America!"[5]

Ries says that when he first saw the Snuggie ad, he found the idea so laughable that he was sure it was a hoax or a joke, just like the Ice Cream Glove. His point in sharing these videos is that you cannot know in advance how the market will react to your new product or service. "Most entrepreneurs, when they are pitching their products to investors, to potential partners, and even to future employees," he writes, "sound just like Ali G pitching the Ice Cream Glove: in love with their own thinking, the amazing product features they are going to build—and utterly out of touch with reality."[6] Your best plans, predictions, and upfront analyses are meaningless unless, and until, they are validated by customer behavior.

Wernher von Braun, the famous NASA rocket scientist, said "one test result is worth one thousand expert opinions," a principle that applies perfectly to the startup journey. "You cannot figure out what products create value for customers at the whiteboard," Eric Ries writes, "where all you have to draw on are opinions." To avoid sinking all of your resources into a nonviable idea, Ries urges new entrepreneurs to get "out of the building" as early as possible and expose their concept to actual customers, to the fact-based scrutiny of the marketplace.[7]

Iteration is an indispensable tool for putting your startup on a discovery-driven track. As shown in Figure 6-2, the basic cycle of iteration is not hard to grasp. An idea leads to action, which leads to a result that can be evaluated. You try something; you observe or measure the outcome; and you develop a new and improved idea to carry into the next iteration. This cycle will look familiar to those with experience in the continuous improvement or lean production movements (echoing the Plan-Do-Check-Act cycle and similar frameworks).

Figure 6-2. The basic cycle of iteration.

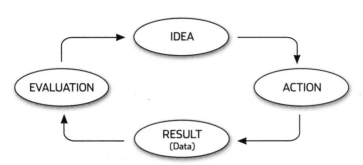

Note that the iteration cycle echoes the core pattern of the *passion trap*, as described in Chapter Two, providing clues as to why highly enthusiastic founders often fail to effectively iterate. First, founders fall in love with their original idea and strive to perfect it, putting most of their resources into the idea step. "We know this is a great idea," the thinking goes, "Why do we need a trial or a proof-of-concept? Let's put smart people and plenty of money behind it, design it just right, and go to market with a bang."

Second, if iteration does occur, the founding team's commitment to their solution can lead to a weak evaluation step in which founders show little interest in unedited customer feedback and deny or rationalize negative feedback received. For these reasons, a vital distinction exists between superficial iteration, going through the motions with little to show for it, and *healthy iteration*, which is like the shedding of a skin. Dead ideas and unworkable strategies are cast aside to make way for the stronger core. As Ries observes, "within every bad idea is a kernel of truth."[8] Successful iteration discovers this truth.

CYCLES OF ITERATION OCCUR AT MULTIPLE LEVELS

An important principle of healthy startup iteration is that it occurs at many levels, beyond simply cranking out new features or products. By "levels," I'm referring to the relative scope and scale of a potential change. At the fast-cycle, narrow end of the spectrum are *feature-level iterations,* adding wrinkles to existing offerings. These can include changes in functionality, size, color, and many other aspects of a product. At the longer-cycle, broader end of the spectrum are *identity-level iterations* that lead to a shift in the entire venture's purpose and identity. A florist, for example, begins sharing space on its delivery vans with other retailers and within a few years has morphed into a full-fledged transportation and home delivery company. This kind of identity shift occurs over longer time horizons and typically has a more seismic impact than a feature-level iteration.

Figure 6-3 provides an example of how various levels of iteration relate to one another in a typical venture. Levels shown here include *features, products/services, systems/processes, strategy, business model,* and *identity.* Let's look at examples of each.

Figure 6-3. Levels of iteration.

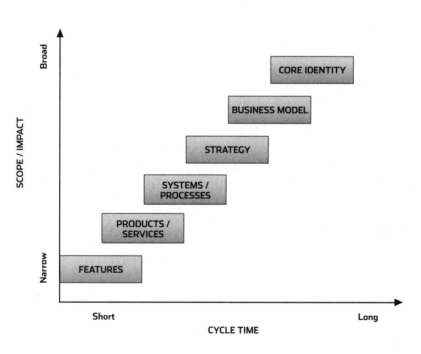

FEATURES – This includes any attempt to enhance or otherwise re-shape an existing product or service. Eric Ries and other developers often refer to making feature-level changes as "shipping code." He notes that, in the early days of IMVU, the virtual chat and social net-working site, he and his team would ship new code many times a day, putting new features in the hands of users and instantly tracking the response.[9] This kind of continual interaction with early adopters cre-ates a learning and development cycle that can dramatically reduce early-stage venture risk. It allows the product or service to be shaped by real user feedback and data, rather than by laboratory speculation or wishful thinking.

PRODUCTS AND SERVICES – In 2007, as Modality began building pro-totypes of its first products, Mark Williams and co-founder Nate O'Keefe began locking up rights to publisher-owned educational content. At the time, they had opinions but no hard facts about what kinds of content iPod owners would covet in digital form, so they hedged their bets by securing rights along a wide spectrum. These included *Netter's Anatomy* for medical students, *BrainQuest* for grade school kids, *Princeton Review* SAT test prep for high schoolers, *Cliff's Notes* for college students, *Law in a Flash* for law school students, and *Frommer's Guides* for travelers. Over time, as certain products caught fire and others struggled, it became clear that Modality's early "sweet spot" would be in the health sciences education market, primarily medical and nursing education, the source of more than 80 percent of revenues by the end of 2009. Modality's ability to iterate rapidly at the product level, resulting in a portfolio of more than 140 titles for sale by the spring of 2010, allowed the company to find, cultivate, and better understand its growing core customer base of healthcare students and professionals.

As Eric Ries emphasizes, an early key to venture success is to avoid the tendency to overdesign your first product—avoiding the mistake of assuming you know what the customer wants—and, in-stead, get early prototypes in the hands of customers who can use, enjoy, kick, or otherwise tear them apart. His phrase for this early of-fering is the "minimum viable product." A minimum viable product is that version of a new product that allows you to learn as much as possible about the customer with the least amount of effort and resources. This approach is not about pulling a few prospective users into a focus group. It requires that you put something up for sale, find out who will buy it, and then rapidly iterate from that starting point.[10]

In contrast to this notion of rapidly iterating a minimally designed product, Lynn Ivey's commitment to the creation of a custom-built adult daycare facility can be understood as a single, expensive, and very long product iteration. Validated learning about customers would have to wait for more than a year as the product was carefully built. The building was an indispensable centerpiece of the business model, but Lynn's resources were dwindling by the time The Ivey finally opened for business.

In the case of The Ivey and other ventures that require a large upfront commitment of time, energy, and capital before a product can be tested in real terms, a key issue is how to test the business hypothesis early, with minimal investment. If, through early testing, a concept proves viable, then more substantial investment can be made with greater confidence. If the original concept does not pan out, alternative concepts can be developed. In The Ivey's case, this might have involved piloting the adult daycare service from a leased space, acquiring early customers and learning about the market until the size of the opportunity clearly merited investment in a new facility. With her chosen approach, Lynn was taking on much more risk, although she and her enthusiastic investors did not necessarily view it as such in the booming Charlotte of 2006. Looking back, Lynn wishes she had mitigated the risk by raising significantly more capital (at least $1 million more) to allow for a slower, steadier customer acquisition and learning process *after* the facility was in place.

SYSTEMS AND PROCESSES – Every time a product or service is delivered, the venture team has an opportunity improve its operational approach and methodology. Core work processes often come together in ad hoc fashion as specific opportunities are chased and captured. This is healthy, in that it connects your operational design to the marketplace and (hopefully) generates cash, but it can also lead to a patchwork of practices that won't scale beyond the first year or two of venture growth.

In the heat of customer demand, healthy iteration and improvement of processes can be challenging. Even though you are painfully aware that you need to improve your delivery system, fifteen more customer orders just came through the door, so you sprint down the existing operational pathway, improvising here and there, vowing to take time later to make necessary fixes and improvements. Of course "later" never comes, and the longer you wait, the more difficult and complex the necessary fixes or improvements become.

As I'll outline in the next section, the key is to establish a regular post-mortem practice, early in your startup trajectory, to look back at each production or delivery cycle, harvest lessons learned, and implement improvements where necessary. In this way, you instill the ethic of continuous improvement into your firm as it grows—the specific learning practices will change, but the *will* to improve is sewn into your venture's DNA.

STRATEGY – Writing about predominantly large corporate organizations, Donald Sull notes the competitive importance of what he calls *strategic agility*, defined as "spotting and seizing game-changing opportunities."[11] This notion of iterating at the strategic level is even more crucial for fledgling ventures that are just beginning to cast innovative products into new or emerging markets. New venture teams can significantly elevate their odds of success by continually assessing broader market opportunities and competitive threats and adapting their strategy where conditions call for change.

In launching D1, J.C. Faulkner and his team planned to open ten lending branches and grow them to the point where each would average $2 million a month in loan volume. After that, the business plan called for expanding the number to twenty branches across the United States, with each branch averaging $2.5 million per month. "When we first got out there," J.C. says, "our branches grew with a lot more focus and a lot faster than we thought they would." As the original branches neared an average of $5 million a month, the D1 team questioned its expansion plan. Why open more lending centers, dilute management focus, and take on more complexity and more leases? "We decided we would try to get our existing ten branches up to $50 million a month," J.C. says. "As it turns out, we got those branches up to $100 million a month, 50 percent faster than we thought we could get the twenty branches up to $2.5 million a month." The result was a more focused and easily coordinated growth strategy, one that wouldn't have been chosen without real-time market feedback.

BUSINESS MODEL – During 2009, even as Modality continued to develop and release exciting new titles for the iPhone, Mark and his team grew increasingly frustrated with the product clutter and noise in the booming AppStore sales channel. Home to more than 100,000 applications and counting, many of them free or very cheap, with names like "Angry Kittens Attack," "Flick-a-Booger," and "Cow Toss," the AppStore had mostly become a distributor of novelties and games rather than a place for serious learners to find educational products. As a result of this low-end chaos in its primary channel, Modality's total sales were climbing more slowly than before, and sales per title were slumping.

While redoubling efforts to improve unit product sales through marketing strategies and a revamped website, Mark and his team decided to quietly launch a complementary "publishing services" model, in which they would sell their production capacity to publishers or other businesses, building new apps in exchange for a negotiated fee. Unlike selling licensed products under the Modality name, this wholesale model was non-speculative, generating cash for every title produced and shifting the market risk and marketing burden to the purchasing client. Early opportunities had already made their way to Modality's doorstep with no marketing, as media companies were looking for ways to compete in the digital space. Mark and his team hoped that they could "turn the knob" and grow this business through more concerted business development efforts. By the spring of 2010, they were enjoying roughly equivalent revenue in each of their two major business lines: the original direct-to-consumer line and newly hatched publishing services.

CORE IDENTITY - The most radical iteration a business can make is to shift its very identity and purpose. Nokia, the communications and mobile phone maker, began as a pulp paper mill in Finland. Texas Instruments started out as an oil exploration service. DuPont, backed by French venture capital, started as a producer of gunpowder. The driving force behind such a change is almost always the discovery of an unanticipated market opportunity that aligns with existing capabilities of the founding team. Returning to the example of Stacy's Pita Chips introduced in Chapter Four, founders Stacy Madison and Mark Andrus abandoned their plans to start a health food restaurant to pursue an unexpected retail opportunity, because customers waiting in line for a sandwich just couldn't keep their hands off of pita chips that had been created as an afterthought. The founders were able to quickly direct their talents and resources to begin capitalizing on the pita chip opportunity and eventually decided to close the original sandwich cart business.

HARVESTING LESSONS USING THE FOUR-QUADRANT FRAMEWORK

For an early-stage venture, the question, "What have we learned?" is more important than the question, "What have we done?" As you bring your concept to life, you will move along a learning curve that takes you from passionate belief in your idea to a more basic understanding of how it plays out in the real world. You get to experience your idea in motion. But how do you make sense of all the information available? How do you separate the signal from the noise and harvest the right lessons amid the often-overwhelming stress and urgency of the startup path?

The four-quadrant framework provides a useful filter to direct and balance your learning across four domains that drive new venture success. Gathering facts, generating insight, and reducing uncertainty in these four areas will reduce your risk and help you position for growth. Build a consistent practice of coming up for air to review your plan and evaluate progress. You can concentrate your learning in the four buckets below, using the suggested questions to stimulate and guide your learning process. Treat these questions as starter list, revising and adding to suit your situation.

FOUNDER – As the old saying goes, be careful what you wish for. Many aspiring founders are surprised along their startup journey to learn that the role they envisioned for themselves is not what it was cracked up to be. To ensure that your passion and skills are aligned with your startup challenge, periodically revisit the questions related to *founder readiness* outlined in Chapter Three with an eye toward what has changed and what is being learned.

- What are you learning about yourself as a founder and entrepreneur? What are you learning about your founding team? What has been most surprising to you, and how can you apply these insights going forward?

- What have you learned about your passion? Do you feel the "fire in the belly" or a "weight on the shoulders"? What factors contribute to each?

- Are you on a path to satisfy your core purpose for making the entrepreneurial leap? Have your reasons and goals shifted? If so, how and why?

- Where is the emerging fit between your skills, experience, personality, etc. and the requirements of your new venture?

- How can you better deploy your strengths and cover for your gaps? How are your core team's strengths and weaknesses playing out in the venture process?

- Are you bringing your best energy, focus, and performance to your venture? If not, what factors stand in the way and how can you best address them?

MARKET – Without a ready market there will be no venture, so finding your market sweet spot is the primary purpose of early iteration. Here are a few specific questions to ensure that you hear and make sense of what the market has to say.

- What have you learned about your core customer? Who are they? Who are they not? What motivates them to use your product or service? How are they using it, and what value are they deriving?

- What have you learned (or what has changed) about the overall market opportunity? What new opportunities and threats are emerging and how might you respond?

- What have you learned about competitors? Who is succeeding in your space and why?

- What factors are driving sales (or lack of sales)? What is working or not working about your customer acquisition process?

- How can you best differentiate your venture and your offerings, based on what you have learned? What is your clearest competitive advantage at this time?

MATH - Once you are up and running and are delivering products and paying suppliers, you can begin to better understand the economic viability of your concept as it plays out in the real world.

- How has your math story played out so far, compared to the plan? What are you learning about the basic economics underlying your business model and strategy?

- What key planning and financial assumptions underlie your model and how are these testing out? How might your plans change as a result?

- What are you learning about the dynamics of profitability and return ($R = M \times V$, from Chapter Five), and what feasible opportunities to increase returns are emerging?

- What have you learned about your venture's ability to generate cash? How are cash reserves relative to your plan?

- What have you learned about required resources and capabilities going forward? How might this impact your strategy, costs, and timelines?

- What is working well or not working well about your approach to financial planning and controls? How well are you staying on top of the numbers?

EXECUTION – Getting things done in a startup environment tends to be more difficult than new founders expect. A key aspect of your new venture learning curve is mastering the elements that must come together to execute on the business plan and strategy.

- *Talent.* Where are strengths and gaps in terms of talent? Are the right people in the right roles to propel the venture forward?

- *Systems and processes.* What's working well in these areas and where are weaknesses or vulnerabilities? What has been learned about technology opportunities and risks?

- *Teamwork.* What are you learning about the role of teamwork in accomplishing the venture's goals? Where is tight teamwork necessary and where should people run independently?

- *Communication.* What communication patterns have developed within and outside the venture? Are goals and priorities clear? Are tough issues being discussed candidly with the right people in the room? If not, why not?

- *Alignment.* How well are the goals and interests of key stakeholders aligned with the goals and priorities of the business? Where are areas of misalignment—where personal motivations or needs are in conflict with the business need—and how can these areas be better aligned?

STAY THE COURSE OR CHANGE DIRECTION: PRINCIPLES FOR MAKING TOUGH CALLS

Rapid iteration builds agility into your business, but it's important to remember that iteration doesn't always mean change. Iteration means executing on an idea and then evaluating the result. Sometimes the result will suggest staying the course. Some ventures iterate along steady, stable paths where the costs of changing direction seem to outweigh the value of the change. When dealing with higher-level issues involving major new products, systems, strategies, or business models, entrepreneurs face both higher stakes and unclear choices. As Arthur Rock, a seasoned entrepreneur and venture capitalist, wrote in his classic 1987 *Harvard Business Review* article, "There's a thin line between refusing to accept criticism and sticking to your guns."[12]

Here are a few principles that apply to the challenge of how to make tough calls when faced with difficult forks in the startup road:

- *Establish a balanced set of decision-making criteria* that reflect your longer-term goals and the fundamentals of venture success. Before becoming attached to a potential solution, ground yourself in what you are trying to accomplish and what is most important for the overall venture. A few examples: How does the potential change align with your passion, purpose, and capabilities as a founder? How well does it align with market realities? How does it perform from a customer and market perspective? How will it impact cash flow and your overall math story? How easy or difficult will it be to successfully execute?

- *Strive to generate multiple alternatives from which to choose,* rather than impulsively going with the first change or solution that comes to mind. It usually takes little time to generate and consider additional options, and this almost always improves the quality of the decision.

- *Distinguish facts from opinions.* As you consider and discuss your options, flag assertions or assumptions not supported by data. While intuition plays a valuable role in informing your choices, be clear about what data are available to either support or disconfirm your "gut."

- *Design experiments or pilots to gather additional data* and work out kinks. Even the most sweeping decisions can usually be tested first on a smaller scale. Rather than committing to a major new partner, for example, try selling and delivering a few projects together to test compatibility.

- *Preserve future flexibility where possible.* Not all commitments are created equal when it comes to future implications. Will this choice lock up a major chunk of your resources with no ability to adapt? Consider how best- and worst-case scenarios might play out over the longer term and how you can weather and adapt to problematic outcomes.

- *Delay important decisions until the last responsible moment.* This is a popular principle among technologists and system designers, who understand the importance of decisiveness in the startup environment. But additional time often brings new data or information that can substantially transform the quality of a solution or a choice, so allow critical choices to "season" as time allows.

CHAPTER SEVEN

Integrity of Communication
Your Secret Startup Weapon

"They are simple tools, and almost all children are adept in their use by the age of ten. Yet presidents and kings will often forget to use them, to their own downfall. The problem lies not in the complexity of these tools but in the will to use them."

—M. Scott Peck, *The Road Less Traveled*

The simplest principles for new venture success are sometimes the hardest to put into practice. Most entrepreneurs and investors will agree that getting the facts about a situation—good, bad, or ugly— is more important than being proved right, and the value of honestly airing differences far outweighs the discomfort it might cause. Yet many of these same venture teams operate from within feel-good bubbles, where perceptions and conversations are distorted by politeness or prejudgment, and where early biases harden into unquestioned dogma.

Cognitive biases are as plentiful as they are powerful, so it's not surprising that blind spots develop quickly and naturally during the startup journey. Feel-good conversations are like comfort food for new venture teams, reinforcing early beliefs and feeding optimism and confidence. When adversity intrudes, as it always does, teams not accustomed to skillfully confronting reality are ill prepared to respond swiftly and smartly. Passion-trapped founders tend to panic instead of lead.

This chapter focuses on how to minimize the overly optimistic distortion of reality that can occur early in the venture formation process, avoid getting trapped in the feel-good bubble, cultivate clarity of thought and discussion, and encourage candor and healthy debate, all while maintaining the positive energy and enthusiasm for your venture. Investing in these outcomes is important, not only as a preventive mechanism, a kind of insurance policy against the risks of unchecked passion, but also as a sound competitive strategy. For venture teams that are smart and disciplined enough to cultivate it, integrity of communication can provide a differentiating advantage in the typical entrepreneurial marketplace, where barriers to entry are often low and success requires outthinking, outhustling, and outmanaging the competition.

Integrity of communication is a straightforward concept, easy to understand yet hard to master. It means embracing the raw reality of your venture, in all its glory and with all its warts. It means that anything is discussable, that conversations include relevant data and opinion, and that new information is welcomed without regard to whether it is "good news" or "bad news." In a high-integrity atmosphere, there is no such thing as bad news, because every piece of data adds to a more complete picture, a clearer, stronger base from which to decide and act.

No One Is Immune to Reality Distortion

During the launch and early growth of D1, J.C. Faulkner and his management team spent a lot of time together in very close quarters. They met every Monday afternoon for five or more hours to scrutinize the past week's accomplishments and the coming week's plans. They debated decisions, monitored results, and held each other accountable for progress. "In those meetings," J.C. says, "we learned how to laugh, we learned how to argue, and we learned how to disagree—all with trust."

By the standards of most leadership teams, the D1 team was hitting on all cylinders. But J.C. knew that even the closest and smartest of teams sometimes avoid critical but uncomfortable topics. For that reason, every few months he and his team would meet with Ken Macher, a San Francisco–based consultant, who specializes in helping groups communicate effectively about their most critical issues. Macher's multi-day sessions with the team aimed to uncover hidden assumptions, focusing as much on what was *unsaid* as on what was said, and his sessions usually revealed concerns that had escaped open discussion and scrutiny.

To prepare for a July 1998 work session, Macher asked each team member to document a recent conversation that he or she had found frustrating or challenging. He asked them to write their learning cases in two columns, with the right-hand column containing a word-for-word record of what each person had said, as it might appear in a movie script. In the left-hand column, the case writer would document what was *not* said, the unshared thoughts and feelings during the conversation. Macher had used this "Left-Hand Column" exercise as a learning tool in previous sessions, so team members knew that their cases might be openly discussed with the full team.[1]

Doug Crisp, D1's head of operations, prepared a case that described a conversation between him and J.C. about growing problems at Home Free Mortgage, their recently launched sister company. Doug had been trying to convince J.C. for some time that the fledgling business was in real danger. He thought its management team was too inexperienced to deal with the current market downturn (it had refused his attempts to help), and the business was hemorrhaging cash. He was not the only person worried. "A number of people had severe concerns about Home Free," Ken Macher recalls, "but were not bringing it up because it was perceived as J.C.'s pet project." Uncharacteristically, J.C. had largely dismissed Doug's concerns, thinking Doug had a personality conflict with Home Free's president and, therefore, couldn't see the situation objectively.

Ken Macher read Doug's case a few days before the session and sensed that it was the tip of an iceberg. He told J.C. he wanted to share it with the full team to start the meeting, and J.C. agreed.

The case immediately struck a nerve. "When we handed out the case and everybody started to read it," Macher says, "It's one of the few times I can remember that a hush fell over the team. It was like . . . *uh-oh.*" J.C. later joked about what the team was probably thinking at that moment: *We're on sacred ground now. We're really going to test these stupid theories.*

No other cases were discussed that day. The rest of the session was devoted to detailed discussion and analysis of the Home Free situation. In the best of environments, Home Free might have stood a chance, but the plummeting mortgage markets were causing the startup to lose $2 million per month, and, more ominously, the same markets were sapping D1's core earnings with no clear end in sight. Home Free's management team, lost in their own feel-good bubble, had been giving J.C. a far too optimistic spin on things. "They believed in what they were doing," J.C later said. "They were too inexperienced to see that the thing had failed." Although he had sunk a tremendous amount of time and personal capital into the venture, J.C. knew it was time to stop the bleeding. He met with Home Free's management team that night to tell them he was closing the venture down.

The Home Free tale is a story of miscalculation and loss, but it would have been much worse had the D1 team not come clean about the gravity of the situation. An optimist by nature, J.C. admits that his emotional attachment to Home Free was causing him to distort the harsh reality of the situation. His team provided a wakeup call, allowing him to see the situation more objectively. Ken Macher, who has observed a lot of leadership teams and organizational cultures, says that the D1 team's discussion about Home Free was a "poster child" for a productive, high-integrity conversation. "A number of things led to it," he says. "The culture of the D1 team had developed to the point that people would bring up an 'un-discussable' topic (with Macher's help, in this case) and the CEO would invite it to be discussed. And that was only the beginning, because they had to work through a lot of fog." Drawing on trust and skill developed as a team, they cut through layers of confusion, clarified what was happening, and decided what needed to be done.

Integrity of Communication: The Basics

In a new venture environment, every choice sets a tone and initiates a pattern. What is talked about, what is avoided, how tough issues are raised and resolved, all of these decisions plant seeds for your future culture, which will eventually grow into a force beyond easy control. "As a parent, or as an entrepreneur, you begin imprinting your beliefs from Day One, whether you realize it or not," writes Howard Schultz, founder of Starbucks. "If you have made the mistake of doing business one way for five years, you can't suddenly impose a layer of different values upon it. By then, the water's already in the well, and you have to drink it."[2]

Instead of directly tackling tough issues, many venture teams surrender to a psychological pressure to do the opposite. A kind of beggar's mentality takes hold of new founders, who are so grateful for support from partners and investors that they shrink from delivering bad news or raising thorny topics. They want to seem—they want to *be*—on top of things, so a lot of energy goes into posturing, instead of seeking the truth. The paradoxical result is that the most critical topics are the least likely to see the light of day. As Ken Macher observes, "the thing that people feel most sheepish about bringing up is often the very thing that needs to be discussed."

Numerous books and careers have been dedicated to the practice of healthy human communication. But a few core principles, outlined below, will determine whether you create early patterns of open communication and plant the seeds of a high-integrity culture.

DON'T CONFUSE GOOD FEELINGS WITH PROGRESS

One by-product of entrepreneurial passion—and the Motivational Media that feed it—is that too many founding teams behave as if positive emotion indicates forward movement. If we walk out of a meeting feeling great, the thinking goes, then things must be on track.

Conversely, people who scrutinize or question progress are cast as negative or disloyal. Doubt is an enemy to be banished. But every new venture journey is fraught with real risks and real threats. Doubts and fears, when properly prioritized and evaluated, lead us to issues that desperately need attention. "Startups are right to be paranoid," says Y Combinator's Paul Graham. "But they sometimes fear the wrong things."[3]

The tendency toward positive packaging gives rise to a familiar shell game between entrepreneurs and investors in which founding teams feel obliged to amplify the good and sanitize the bad. But smart investors know that rosy early-phase reports don't equate to value creation. Chris Holden remembers how impressed he and his colleagues at Court Square Ventures were when Mark Kahn raised what could be considered bad news immediately after finalizing their investment deal. "One of the reasons his business took off so fast is that he had no pride about coming back to us five minutes after the ink was dry on our deal, saying 'I think I might have misjudged this piece of the equation and we need to change it this way or that way.'" In countless other deals, Chris has seen his share of founders who won't acknowledge issues that need to be addressed. "They don't want to go back to their investors with anything that makes them look like they weren't perfectly prescient, with perfect foreknowledge, or anything that makes it look like things are shaky underfoot," he says. "But in reality, what the investor craves is the opposite. Because you *know* that things are going to be shaky underfoot, and you're on shifting sands always. What you want to see is their reaction."

Adversity is more than an inevitable companion in your venture formation process. It is often a sign that you are focusing on knotty problems that need to be untangled. Turbulence builds entrepreneurial muscle and opens windows into your team's talent, character, and commitment. Mastery in any field comes through tough stretches of grinding and problem solving, and the path to sustained venture success is no different. For the most part, value creation is the result of unglamorous day-to-day toil, not satisfying high-five moments.

INVEST TIME TO CULTIVATE INTEGRITY

As noted in this book's introduction, the much-sought-after secrets of entrepreneurial success are not so secret. They are known to most founders, which begs the question: *Why do we, as founders, not do what we know to be good for us? What gets in the way of doing the right things?* I'm convinced that a major obstacle is the unrelenting urgency and haste—the perceived lack of time—that dominates most startup environments. It can be argued that time is a founder's most precious resource. Infusing your venture with high-integrity communication requires the use of this resource. Venture-changing conversations can't always be scheduled in advance or put on a convenient agenda, and they don't lend themselves to hurried shortcuts.

Social psychological research supports the idea that hurriedness is a major culprit in our lack of attention to things we say we value. In a famous study conducted in 1973 at Princeton University, John M. Darley, a professor of social psychology, and doctoral student C. Daniel Batson researched the phenomenon of "Good Samaritan" behavior. They wanted to know what kinds of personality traits and situational factors influence a person's likelihood of stopping to help an obviously distressed victim. In the study, they asked seminary students to walk across campus, one at a time, to a building where they would give a presentation. En route, each subject encountered a man (an actor) in obvious need of help, slumped in a doorway, moaning and coughing. The question of interest was: Which students would stop to help and why?

Upon analyzing the results, the researchers were surprised to find no relationship between subjects' personalities and whether or not the individuals would stop to help the victim. Instead, helping behavior was mostly tied to a single variable: the degree to which subjects were in a hurry. Of those subjects who were told they had plenty of time to arrive at their presentation site, 63 percent stopped and rendered aid to the victim. People who were told they had a few minutes to spare stopped 45 percent of the time. And a third group of subjects, those who were told that they were already running late to their presentations, stopped only 10 percent of the time, even though they passed very close to the victim (a few even stepped over him on the way to their destination).[4]

The message of the Good Samaritan study is that our sense of urgency can greatly influence whether our actions match up with our espoused values and priorities. The "hurried" seminary students in the study would claim to be just as altruistic as the other participants, but their sense of urgency clearly diminished their ability to act according to their stated values. Similarly, many entrepreneurs intend to create highly functioning, well-communicating teams but often cast these good intentions aside amid the time pressures of a startup environment, where an ever-growing list of urgent concerns and to-dos crowds out more fundamental issues.

J.C. Faulkner, when asked about his tactics for building trust and cohesiveness among his management team, concurs with the idea of no shortcuts. "It's real simple," he says. "It took time. Trust is not something that you can buy, or that happens quickly. It is an intense thing that has to be developed over time." The paradoxical good news for D1 was that this investment of time led to terrific speed and growth. "We had a goal to produce $40 million of business in a three-year period," J.C. recalls, "and we did it in twelve months. In my wildest dreams, I wouldn't have thought it would happen, but I learned that an efficient management team that trusts each other can make so many decisions. The question is: How quickly, how effectively can you have conversations to make the best decisions? Some teams are too slow in making decisions, and some are very quick to make bad decisions. But if you are fast *and* you make the right decisions, it's explosive."

SURROUND YOURSELF WITH SMART PEOPLE

Another hallmark of J.C. Faulkner's approach to building D1 was that he sought and attracted the highest level of talent. Doug Crisp and other members of his management team left senior posts and promising careers with one of the largest banks in the United States to join D1. As they attracted others to the venture, a positive talent cycle took hold, where talented people created an energetic, achievement-driven culture, which attracted even more high performers. J.C. soon realized that the high level of talent at D1 had the unexpected effect of reinforcing open communication and accountability. "The danger of hiring very smart people," he says, "is you can't 'spin' things to them even if you want to. You are held accountable."

Likewise, as a new founder, you can lessen your susceptibility to the passion trap by partnering with the smartest, most talented people available, people who are driven to succeed, who can discern fact from opinion, who will tell you the truth, and, most important, who care more about the good of the venture than keeping you comfortable. These benefits are additive to the more fundamental fact that the quality of your core team will drive your ability to create value over time. "Your biggest challenge will be building a great team," says John Doerr of the powerhouse VC firm Kleiner, Perkins, Caulfield & Byers. "In the world today, there's plenty of technology, plenty of entrepreneurs, plenty of money—what's in short supply is great teams. Focus on the team. Teams win."[5]

It helps to include a few cage-rattlers on your extended team, people who will speak in unedited language and who don't suffer fools gladly. Cage-rattlers are not the savviest communicators, but you will always know what they think. "It is very difficult for the strong-willed entrepreneur to really listen to critics," writes Daniel Isenberg, professor of management science at Babson College. "If you find people who will be painfully honest with you, get them on board."[6] These might include co-founders, team members, prospective or actual investors, advisers, mentors, or old high school buddies who have seen you at your worst, as well as early-adopting customers who relish the right to complain about your offerings after surrendering their hard-earned money. Whatever their role, the cage-rattler's essential qualification is an unedited propensity to poke holes in your plan, ask tough questions, and raise worrisome possibilities.

RAISE THE QUALITY OF CONVERSATIONS

Building on pioneering work from the field of organizational learning by theorists and practitioners such as Chris Argyris, Peter Senge, and

Robert Putnam, consultant Ken Macher developed expertise and tools for helping business teams dramatically improve discussions and decisions, and he brought the full force of these ideas to D1's early growth process. Conversations became a unit of focus for D1's leadership team and a powerful point of leverage for increasing capacity throughout the venture. "I began to realize that the quality of conversations is not only indicative of the culture," he says, "it *creates* culture, and it determines the quality of decision-making, planning, everything."

In Appendix B, I have included a list of helpful resources and tools for improving the quality of conversations that will drive the success of your venture. Here are a few principles and guidelines to keep in mind:

- *Frame conversations as a pathway to team intelligence.* Some startup founders are hesitant to spend time building interpersonal clarity and chemistry, because they fear it will be seen as a touchy-feely exercise more suited for an episode of NBC's *The Office* than a startup environment. Counteract this concern by positioning high-quality conversations as a non-negotiable business imperative, a way to elevate your team's collective IQ and performance. Most of your competitors' half-hearted efforts at teamwork will result in a net loss of capacity; their whole will be less valuable than the sum of individual parts. Tight teamwork will give you a competitive advantage and a more reliable path to value creation.

- *Use targeted involvement.* One of the skills in creating productive conversations is knowing who to involve, when to involve them, and why. Be careful to include people who bring key expertise to a decision or who will play a major role in implementing it, but don't make the mistake of involving everyone in everything. I've known a few founders whose teams became unnecessarily bogged down in unending consensus-oriented deliberations. These not only were a bad use of most people's time but also led to cynicism about the value of team meetings. Skillful leaders strike a balanced approach to involving others, using multiple channels of communication to keep people in the loop while saving more inclusive conversations for matters that are best resolved in a face-to-face format.

- *Value data.* Communicating with integrity hinges on the ability to distinguish fact from opinion and to infuse decision-making processes with verifiable data and logical thinking. The more passionate you are about a plan or a product, the more vital it is to invite others to scrutinize your facts and your logic. "You're neither right nor wrong because other people agree with you," says Warren Buffett, chairman and CEO of Berkshire Hathaway. "You're right because your facts are right and your reasoning is right, and that's the only thing that makes you right."[7]

- *Encourage team members to share their left-hand columns.* We are all familiar with conversations in which what is talked about is far removed from the unspoken thoughts and feelings that swirl beneath the surface. Sometimes these thoughts are not worth sharing. At other times, they point to issues that desperately need attention. The left-hand column represents all of the data, insight, and emotion that we withhold from others. If you want to elevate the quality of your conversations, you can do so by taking three simple steps: First, become more aware of your unacknowledged thoughts and feelings during key conversations. Second, skillfully share these where relevant. Finally, invite others to do the same.

- *Balance advocacy and inquiry.* In my consulting role with new ventures, I sometimes assess the core team's ability to solve problems and make decisions. I often start by grabbing a notepad and quietly observing the conversational patterns in a team meeting. Everything that is said falls into two categories: *advocacy*, where team members assert, claim, or push for their point of view, or *inquiry*, in which team members seek to understand another person's opinion or gather information about a situation or an issue. Invariably, business discussions are heavy with advocacy, where 80 to 90 percent of the air time is devoted to staking out positions and pushing points of view. This leaves very little room for inquiry, aimed at surfacing and evaluating new data and testing assumptions. And it points to a tremendous learning opportunity for most new venture teams: to promote more frequent inquiry into the thinking of others and to cultivate more skillful methods of advocacy, such as revealing the logic underlying an assertion or inviting others to scrutinize one's logic and add new perspectives to it.[8]

OVERCOMMUNICATE

In a fast-paced startup environment, it's easy for founders to develop lazy or sloppy communication habits and to think team members are up-to-date on emerging issues when they are not. Integrity of communication means ensuring that all relevant people are kept in the loop, and that you, as a founder, are aware of the ideas, concerns, and opportunities in orbit around you. Healthy communication is a multidirectional process, an infinite loop of outgoing and incoming data and meaning. Although each conversation is a building block, it pays to put broader practices and mechanisms in place early in your startup process to knit together information and thinking across the venture. These can include daily or weekly huddles, email updates, regular phone calls, lunches or happy hours, and, of course, meetings of all varieties. It's popular in today's leadership literature to slam meetings as a perversion of human nature, to be avoided at all costs. But problems with meetings always stem from controllable factors, and anyone who says they hate meetings can also recall a few that they enjoyed and benefited from. The solution is not to eliminate meetings, but to ensure that they are judiciously scheduled, well planned, and efficiently led.

Overcommunicating does *not* mean communicating everything that comes to mind, but rather clarifying what core messages need to be shared, then repeating these with numbing regularity. J.C. Faulkner is known as a charismatic speaker, but his outgoing communication style during D1's growth years was surprisingly simple and redundant. This was by design. In regular monthly meetings with his entire staff, he would recap D1's direction and priorities by addressing three basic questions: *Where have we been? Where are we now? Where are we going (and why)?* In the next month's session, he would follow the same format, adapting his comments to reflect any changes. And if you bumped into him in the hallway at any point in between, his thoughts would follow the same familiar pattern. His goal was to ensure that every single person in the venture was fully informed about his intentions and his thinking. He believed the stakes related to overcommunicating were far too high to leave this to chance.

In every interaction, J.C. was also intently focused on gathering new data and learning from others. He reserved a quarter of his time for working on communication and culture throughout the business and would often circulate among employees at all levels and in all areas. A gifted conversationalist who quickly put people at ease, he usually appeared to be simply shooting the breeze. He was, but he also followed a consistent process of asking questions to understand the guts of the growing business from the ground up. His ready grasp of D1 from top to bottom, which seemed to come so naturally, was the hard-earned result of his commitment to overcommunication. "I have heard a lot of business leaders say they wanted to make communication an underpinning of their company," observes Bob Tucker, J.C. Faulkner's long-time business attorney. "I have never seen anyone focus on it to the degree that D1 focused on it, and I think it is easy to underestimate how much effort it takes to create good thinking. Communication is a very, very effective way to enhance the odds of that coming about."

Four Personal Tools for Bursting the Feel-Good Bubble

Integrity of communication starts at the personal level with the fundamental issue of how a founder deals with incoming data and opinion. The most reliable predictor of your venture's future climate is your own outlook and behavior. So, if you aim to set a tone for healthy communication and minimize the distortion of reality within your new business, start with yourself. I have found that a core set of personal attributes, *curiosity, humility, candor,* and *scrutiny,* will lay a foundation for truth-telling and create a ripple effect that drives healthy relationships with co-founders, team members, investors, and other business partners.

CURIOSITY

Jim Collins, the bestselling author and renowned student of business leadership, has observed that all creative and entrepreneurial endeavors require "the precision of a scientist and the wonder of a child."[9] Successful entrepreneurs and investors tend to have ravenous appetites for new knowledge and are persistently curious about what newly discovered data might mean. They crave objective sources of information, but are curious, too, about the subjective opinions of other people—their customers, investors, and team members—especially when these opinions clash with their own. Instead of shrinking back or tuning out when faced with a differing point of view, the curious entrepreneur leans forward and invites the speaker to elaborate. Their intellectual posture is not one of knowing, but of questioning: *What am I missing? What does this person see or understand that I don't? What do these data suggest about the path forward?* The insatiable nature of this brand of curiosity means that the entrepreneurial learning curve never ends. The more one learns, the greater the appetite to learn more. Malcolm S. Forbes, longtime publisher of *Forbes* magazine, could have been talking about entrepreneurial curiosity when he said, "Education's purpose is to replace an empty mind with an open one."[10]

But founders who have fallen in love with an idea are usually looking for assurance instead of illumination. In his well-circulated list, *17 Mistakes Startups Make,* John Osher, seasoned entrepreneur and creator of hundreds of consumer products, highlights a root cause of startup derailment: *Seeking confirmation of your actions rather than seeking the truth.* "You want to do something," he says, "so you talk to people who work for you. You talk to family and friends. But you're only looking for confirmation: You're not looking for the truth. You're looking for somebody to tell you you're right."[11]

As we saw in Chapter One, most aspiring entrepreneurs collect affirmations like a teenager collects text messages. Constructive, sugar-free criticism is hard to find, even when you crave it, so if you're looking for validation instead, you will certainly find it. And when you finally encounter the rare, no-holds-barred critique of your idea, you might bristle and defend against it, rather than openly consider its meaning.

Lynn Ivey looks back at her early planning for The Ivey and remembers having little patience for people who raised concerns or pointed out risks to her plan. Because she was already locked into a path to construct a world-class facility, her focus was on evangelizing the concept and raising funds. She couldn't fully contemplate the possibility that her model might have significant flaws. The train had left the station, so to speak, and she needed affirmation and positive ideas, not skepticism or debate.

In particular, she recalls how the former CEO of a major healthcare system told her he believed The Ivey would have trouble competing with the established in-home care services in the area. Looking back, Lynn wishes she had been more curious about his concerns and probed for more insight, but, at the time, she wrote him off as a somewhat combative curmudgeon, someone who didn't understand her vision.

HUMILITY

Humility is the opposite of hubris and serves as its antidote. No amount of passion and expertise will eliminate your blind spots or protect you from mistakes. To the contrary, your enthusiasm for an idea is more likely to narrow your field of attention and accentuate the risk of blindness. You cannot know in your startup's earliest stage what the customer will want, what the markets will reward, how competitors will behave, or what unpredictable twists and turns the future will bring. Accepting this reality is the essence of humility.

Warren Buffett, regarded as one of history's best business minds, knows that his own carefully honed judgment is permanently fallible. In his 2007 annual letter to shareholders (the net worth of his firm increased by $12.3 billion that year) he outlined a series of mistakes. "And now it's confession time," he wrote. "It should be noted that no consultant, board of directors, or investment banker pushed me into the mistakes I will describe. In tennis parlance, they were all unforced errors." He goes on to explain in detail a couple of questionable investment decisions. "The only explanation is that my brain had gone on vacation and forgot to notify me," he writes. "One thing is for sure. I'll make similar mistakes in the future."[12]

The day after J.C. Faulkner and his management team decided to close down Home Free was an exercise in humility. "It was one of those unforgettable moments when I had to acknowledge my mistake and lay off ninety-five people in one day, which was the hardest thing I ever had to do," J.C. says. "Then, I got in front of the other hundred people[in D1's home office]. We admitted the challenges in the market. We admitted the mistakes we had made . . . we just came clean. There was no positive spin. I was obviously concerned that I would lose credibility when I explained I was wrong, but what I learned was that people appreciated the honesty. They felt good that we understood our mistakes; and it kind of humanized us a little bit."

An investor friend of mine once explained to me why he was willing to stand behind the expansion plans of a young restaurateur. "He's young and passionate; he has great ideas and an incredible work ethic," he said. "But the thing that sets him apart is his humility. Although he knows a lot about the restaurant business and he has great instincts, you would never know it from how he interacts with people. He is a learning machine, and he is incredibly driven to find out what other people know. He has surrounded himself with highly experienced people, people who have accomplished great things in the industry, and he becomes a student at their feet—*teach me, show me, help me understand what I can learn from you.*"

CANDOR

J.C. Faulkner remembers a very early source of advice about the value of honesty: "My grandfather—he was a coal miner—he said something about integrity and truth that I've never forgotten. He said that the very moment you feel like you have to lie; when you feel like you want to be untruthful; when you're so scared to tell somebody the truth; when there's that much at stake, that's the very moment you *have* to tell the truth. The fact you feel like you want to lie validates how important the truth is. It validates that you are dealing with a real issue, something that is only going to get worse."

Founders who say they value candor will eventually be tested as to whether they mean it. One of the sternest and most unpleasant examples of this is the common need to confront performance problems, to deal with team members who are not cutting it. Nearly every team, it seems, has a member or two who are not performing up to par, or who have burned too many interpersonal bridges, and whose struggles are commonly known and discussed throughout the venture (except when they are around). Mark Williams remembers the sinking feeling in his stomach when he fully realized that a key team member was no longer a good fit for Modality's growth needs. After a period of agonizing about how to address the situation, he was able to candidly share his thinking with the person and negotiate a fair deal to transition him out of the business. As in many such cases, the exiting team member appreciated the integrity of the process and was somewhat relieved to no longer be straining in a role incompatible with his considerable strengths.

When it comes to open communication, you may find that your challenge as an entrepreneur is less about being truthful with others and more about ensuring that others are completely honest with you. With partners and team members, you will likely get back what you project. "I have found that when people see you doing something as a leader over time, that behavior becomes the expected norm," says J.C. "It's what people think they are supposed to do. When you as a leader are completely unedited and candid, about both good and bad things, that candor opens the door for them to follow suit."

You can also increase your odds of getting the truth by explicitly asking for it and then rewarding it through listening and taking appropriate action. Bob Tucker remembers how J.C. set a tone for unvarnished feedback in their working relationship. "One of the first things that J.C. said to me was—and this is one of his favorite expressions: 'I don't know what I don't know. If you see me doing or saying something that you think is a mistake or with which you disagree, then I want to know about it. I may not agree with you, but I want to know where you see it differently.'" J.C. backed up his request with actions over time, demonstrating that he really wanted to hear opposing views (his quick dismissal of Doug Crisp's concerns about Home Free was a notable exception). For his part, Bob Tucker has seen his share of leaders who fail to walk their talk. "I can't tell you how many times I have seen business leaders say it's their objective [to promote candor] when in fact they do nothing to implement it, and I have seen many of them declare it and create the opposite effect, where anybody who disagrees with them gets shot down."

SCRUTINY

Wise entrepreneurs and investors understand that great ventures are forged, not in retreats or laboratories, but on the field of play, where offerings and delivery systems are subject to the eye-opening scrutiny that only the marketplace can provide. For this reason, most highly successful businesses end up looking very different from what founders intended or expected. The creative dynamic here is often like that of the proverbial sausage factory. Even if the end result tastes great, the process for getting there is not always pretty.

As a passionate founder, it is critical that you deal with everyday reality in a way that doesn't sap your confidence and enthusiasm. Successful entrepreneurs are resilient, persevering in the face of adversity, and this fact is sometimes mistakenly interpreted to mean that they race past obstacles by focusing only on the positive aspects of a situation, by seeing the glass as "half full." But skillful entrepreneurs prevail over problems precisely because they acknowledge and address them. They stare down reality every day, traversing tough passages without losing sight of the higher summit to which they aspire. "This is a very important lesson," says Admiral James Stockdale, quoted by Jim Collins in his book *Good to Great*, "You must never confuse faith that you will prevail in the end—which you can never afford to lose— with the discipline to confront the most brutal facts of your current reality, whatever they might be."[13]

In a high-integrity startup environment, everything is open to scrutiny. Founders scrutinize their own thinking and invite the scrutiny of others. This includes the willingness to entertain skeptics and take a systematic look at one's own doubts and fears. Rather than causing a downward spiral of increasing negativity, as positive thinking enthusiasts might argue, I have found this practice of surfacing and evaluating doubts to lead to even higher levels of confidence. It is the business equivalent of a child's leaving the security of the bedcovers to confirm, once and for all, that no monster is hiding under the bed. As Czechoslovakia's heroic former president, Vaclav Havel, once wrote, "Isn't it the moment of most profound doubt that gives rise to new certainties?"[14]

CHAPTER EIGHT

Staying Power

Give Your Venture Time to Take Flight

"It's not that I'm so smart. It's just that I stay with problems longer."

—Albert Einstein

You can do everything well. You can prepare yourself as a founder, aim for a robust market, design an economically sound business model, move forward with flexibility, and surround yourself with straightforward truth-tellers. Still, getting your venture safely off the ground will likely take more of your time, money, and effort than you expect. Most great ideas require time to work, and it may take a long series of sparks to finally create a roaring fire. Just as overnight successes are often decades in the making, "home run" businesses are most often due to the accumulation of many swings at the plate, where founding teams persevere over time to seize opportunities that couldn't have been scheduled, or even anticipated, in advance.

Unfortunately, one of the common side effects of falling in love with a business idea is the founder's assumption that success will come quickly and easily. Due to the nearly universal tendency to over-project early sales and under-project costs, the startup runway can evaporate quickly and dangerously. This is the immediate reason why many ventures fail without ever turning a profit. But it also points to a significant opportunity: Entrepreneurs who do what is necessary to keep their business alive over time, treating time as a competitive advantage rather than a dwindling resource, can dramatically elevate their odds of venture survival and growth. "The first thing we know about being successful as an entrepreneur is: If you can make it through the early years, your odds of success will go way up," writes Scott Shane, professor of entrepreneurial studies at Case Western Reserve University and author of *The Illusions of Entrepreneurship.* Shane cites more than twenty studies, showing that, when it comes to new ventures, "the odds of your new business failing are highest when you first start and decline in relation to the length of time you have been in business. And it isn't just the chance of staying alive that increases over time. The data also show that the average start-up also becomes more profitable as it gets older."[1]

This final chapter will focus on strategies for strengthening your venture's staying power, your ability to keep moving forward. The forces impacting staying power operate at two levels. The first level is that of the venture itself, where factors external to you as a founder will either lengthen your runway or cut it dangerously short. The second set of forces acts at the personal level, where your ability to perform with stamina and persevere over time will ultimately determine your success in building a thriving business over the long haul.

Venture-Level Strategies: Strengthening and Lengthening Your Runway

The metaphor of the runway is widely used among entrepreneurs to represent both the excitement of speeding toward a successful liftoff and the risk of crashing into the heap of floundering ventures just beyond the end of the pavement. What follows are four strategies for building a long, strong runway for your venture.

1. Launch close to the customer.

2. Address your biggest risks early.

3. Raise more money than you think you will need.

4. Commit resources wisely.

LAUNCH CLOSE TO THE CUSTOMER

In every successful startup journey, there is a point of no return, where the aspiring founder moves from the idea stage to whole-hearted commitment to the cause. This passage is always marked by a stepped-up investment of time and resources, and, in some cases, includes resigning from a job to plunge full-time into a new venture role. You are no longer contemplating whether to move forward. You are on the clock, with money falling through the hourglass.

Even after burning significant time and cash, however, many start-ups haven't really started. They have yet to interact with paying customers. They understand very little about market demand. They may not have a ready-to-sell product or a workable channel for sales and distribution. Instead, they are engaged in pre-launch activities, such as conceiving the future business, developing products, building execution plans, recruiting partners, or putting supporting technology in place. These activities are typically necessary, and some types of ventures (life sciences ventures and speculative real estate development, for example) require long, heavily funded pre-launch periods. But pre-launch activities that are not directly aimed at acquiring clients are often several steps removed from the marketplace, the arena in which your venture's viability will ultimately be tested.

Therefore, one of the keys to strengthening your runway is to move your effective starting point, the point at which you plunge in full-time and begin to burn significant resources, as close as possible to your point of revenue creation. This usually means incubating and gestating your idea as inexpensively as you can, while making a living through other means. How much of your idea can you develop and test in advance without a huge commitment of capital? How fully can you develop a working product before you make the full-time plunge?

How well can you research and understand the market for your idea, even pre-selling customers, before you cross the point of no return?

The opportunity here is two-fold. First, you will hit your runway with much more than a raw idea, bringing a keener grasp of your concept and projected path to profitability. Second, the more inexpensively you can answer the above questions, the more capital will be preserved for the critical process of iterating your idea in the real world, allowing you to get your offering in the hands of paying customers, understand their experience, and use this knowledge to improve your fledgling business model. With this approach, you can accelerate down the runway efficiently and with greater focus, instead of spending precious on-the-clock time bouncing untested ideas back and forth.

The most desirable point from which to launch a business is with paying customers already in hand, generating cash from day one. DriveSavers, a $20 million data recovery company based in Novato, California, was pulled into existence by a growing computer-based problem in the mid-1980s. Founders Scott Gaidano and Jay Hagan worked for a company that sold computer hard drives when the firm went bankrupt and closed. Out of work, they began talking about launching a seafood business, but they soon received frantic calls from former customers whose hard drives had crashed. At the time, few people knew how to recover data from fried computers. "There was no manual. Nobody knew how to do it," Gaidano says. As they began helping customers retrieve data, word spread quickly, and a solid business was born.[2]

My first consulting practice was the result of client requests. While working with First Union Corporation in the mid-1990s, I was considering a move to external consulting but needed a bridge, something to help me transition from the security of a regular paycheck to the freedom and uncertainty of self-employment. Late in 1997, I received inquiries from two outside organizations needing consulting help. The resulting projects promised to bring a healthy revenue stream over four to six months, enough time to build a healthy pipeline of future business. These first clients gave me a solid bridge to the outside world and allowed me to set up my consulting practice with confidence.[3]

Although he didn't start with specific clients in hand, J.C. Faulkner serves as an exemplary model for how to study and scrutinize a market idea while working for someone else. In his sales management role with First Union, he developed close relationships with hundreds of entrepreneurs and salespeople throughout the mortgage industry. Before resigning from his job, he knew exactly what customer segments he would target with his new venture and how his early business model would work. Even with this preparation, he spent more than $600,000 in capital over a year's time before breaking even, but because he had patiently allowed his concept to mature prior to launch, he moved his effective starting point much closer to the marketplace than most venture founders.

In contrast, consider the example of two corporate professionals who, talking over a beer on a Friday afternoon, hit upon an idea for providing an innovative information service to large corporations. Within a few weeks, they had resigned their well-paying jobs. They tapped into their personal savings to bring two more salaried team members on board, leased office space for the team, built a prototype of their technology, and began pitching their concept to senior buyers in target organizations. After six months of expenses, as their resources began to diminish, they were still in search of their first account. These founders continue to gamely press on, and their concept may yet catch fire, but their margin for error is now razor thin. Had they chosen to test and refine their concept prior to committing full resources to it, it's likely that they would now enjoy a much lengthier startup runway.

ADDRESS YOUR BIGGEST RISKS EARLY

Venture capitalists call it the Valley of Death, the period after a founder has begun to spend capital but has yet to find a steady stream of revenues. A large percentage of new business attempts never make it through this first phase, which is why startups are known to be hazardous and the word "entrepreneur" conjures an image of a daring, swashbuckling gambler. But, as Matthew J. Eyring and Clark G. Gilbert note in the May 2010 issue of *Harvard Business Review*, the stereotype of the risk-loving entrepreneur is a myth, at least among those who are highly successful. Effective entrepreneurs recognize that some level of risk comes with the new venture territory and is necessary to create value, but they are not the bold risk-takers that they are made out to be. They are, instead, in the authors' words, "relentless managers of risk." They understand that not all risks are created equal, so they identify and prioritize threats that pose the greatest danger to their venture. Gilbert and Eyring call these "deal-killer risks," and wise founders find ways to creatively address these early in the startup process.

Gilbert and Eyring observe that "when risks are overlooked, fewer than 15 percent of firms are still in operation three years after initial funding."[4] An important strategy for lengthening your venture runway is to identify, very early in your planning process, deal-killer risks that might stop you in your tracks. These risks usually correspond to fundamental assumptions and uncertainties that must play out in your favor for your concept to succeed—an expectation of strong market demand, for example, or the availability of key expertise, favorable regulatory changes, or well-functioning technology. Once you have identified the handful of key uncertainties to be addressed, you can then work to reduce the likelihood of their occurring and build contingency plans to deal with them if and when they do occur.

Here are some examples of how successful entrepreneurs have addressed early-stage risks to clear their runway of potentially venture-killing obstacles.

- *Market Risk.* For enthusiastic founders, the most fundamental assumption of all is that an abundance of paying customers will be waiting to buy your product or service as soon as it is released. These expectations are often too rosy, which means that the existence of adequate market demand is almost always a pivotal area of uncertainty for the new venture. You can mitigate this risk through piloting, prototyping, and related approaches, as outlined in Chapters Four and Six.

  A powerful approach for radically reducing market risk is to sell your product before you build it. Starting with $1,000 in funds in 1984, Michael Dell, founder of Dell Computer, launched a build-to-order computer business from his University of Texas dorm room at age 19. To avoid the cost and risks associated with holding an inventory of components and finished products, Dell got his orders from customers up front, and then he secured necessary components to create each customized computer. This approach brought advantages from a cash flow perspective, but its most fundamental value was that it directly tied his incremental investment of resources to the presence of validated customer demand, effectively eliminating market risk from the startup equation.[5]

- *Relationship Risk.* In 2006 and 2007, Mark Williams and his Modality co-founders were developing a technology for delivering content to the Apple iPod that they felt was compatible and secure within the iPod's architecture. Overcoming this technical barrier required them to continue to iterate their software solution, called Modality Manager, but also required Mark to convince key technologists and senior leaders within Apple that Modality's solution was safe and effective. As he wrote in a planning brief in January of 2007, "Currently, Apple developers are uncomfortable with the Modality Manager solution because of potential to cause problems for consumers as the iPod platform evolves."

  The stakes attached to gaining Apple's approval could not have been higher. Modality's offerings were exclusively developed for Apple's vast customer base and designed to fit within Apple's products. Mark's goal was to earn Apple's full support so that the powerful company would embrace and champion Modality and its innovative solutions. But in terms of scale and clout, Modality was the proverbial flea riding on the back of a bear. At a minimum, Mark needed Apple leadership to tolerate his early attempts to integrate his technology with theirs. Anything less would amount to a deathblow.

  Mark focused a great deal of time and energy into strengthening his relationships with key Apple leaders, working to understand their objectives and concerns, and developing solutions that worked for both companies. The approach paid off, as he noted in an e-mail to advisers in late February 2007. "A key development occurred yesterday," he wrote. "Following a meeting between the Worldwide Developers Group and iPod Marketing, it appears that Apple is comfortable enough with our current software solution to work directly with us on distribution in the Apple Retail Stores and in their online channels."[6] Mark's partnership with Apple would continue to improve and mature. Modality developed a reputation within Apple as a talented, trustworthy partner, leading to a host of opportunities over the next few years. Increasingly, Apple championed Modality and its products, and recommended the Modality team to its institutional and educational partners.

- *Operational Risk.* Every entrepreneur's plan contains assumptions about how the product or service will be created and delivered to customers. In the passion and haste of a launch, these assumptions are often untested or unexamined, although they are usually fraught with uncertainty and, in some cases, pose tremendous risks to the venture. Gilbert and Eyring note that these operational risks can often be evaluated in surprisingly simple ways. They cite the example of Reed Hastings, founder of Netflix, the movie-by-mail business, who conducted a simple, early test of his concept's logistical viability: He mailed himself a CD in an envelope. "By the time it arrived undamaged," the authors write, "he had spent 24 hours and the cost of postage to test one of the venture's key operational risks."[7]

  Operational risks can also involve reliance on key personnel. One of my startup clients began as a spinoff from an existing company, having negotiated a deal that allowed it to transport nine major client accounts into the new venture. But until the new company could develop its own technology platform to service the accounts, a task requiring at least six months to complete, the original company's operations team would continue to service the accounts. In my first meeting with the founders of the spinoff, we acknowledged that the dependency on the original company's operation represented a significant area of risk. What if key team members in the original company favored their own client accounts over those that had been transferred? Worse yet, what if one or more key members of the operations team, already stretched to capacity and openly unhappy about the spinoff decision, decided to call it quits? Revenue from the inherited accounts would be important to the new company's startup runway, so any major disruptions to client service could pose serious problems.

The next day, the operations leader in the original company confirmed our fears and submitted her resignation. While not a deal-killing blow, this event required a lot of attention and problem solving from the new team and detracted from other priorities. Fortunately, the team had identified back-up plans for communicating with clients and serving their needs until an in-house platform was up and running.

These are just a few examples of areas of early-stage risk. Each venture will bring its own unique set of uncertainties that can lead to a fatal early blow. To address these, scrutinize and test key aspects of your concept sooner rather than later, even if your entrepreneurial passion and optimism tempt you to assume the best. Eyring and Gilbert note that many venture managers succumb to this temptation. "Instead of testing their assumptions," they write, "they become more and more invested in confirming them. But successful entrepreneurs do the opposite: They devise low-cost experiments to disprove a concept before it's too late."[8]

RAISE MORE MONEY THAN YOU THINK YOU WILL NEED

This section expands upon a principle I shared near the end of Chapter Five, one that directly impacts your available runway and deserves emphasis. Human beings have always been poor predictors of the future. Highly passionate entrepreneurs represent a special case of this phenomenon, routinely favoring rose-colored views of the new venture path, especially when it comes to estimating capital needs. One of the simplest, most important strategies for ensuring that you make it through your earliest phase is to secure more than adequate funding to get your venture to the point where it is self-sustaining.

Even though J.C. Faulkner entered his startup launch with a highly refined understanding of his target market and a well-tuned business plan, he took no chances when it came to funding. "My philosophy," he says, "was that you should raise two-and-a-half times more money than you think you'll ever need in the worst case scenario. This was based on great advice from my dad, who saw a lot of businesses succeed and fail as an accountant." Accordingly, the D1 business plan projected that the company would spend about $800,000 before becoming profitable, so J.C. secured access to $2.5 million before taking his idea to market. About one-fourth of this was in the form of his own career savings, while some money came from private investors (friends and business associates who trusted J.C. and knew his track record in the industry) and the rest came from loans and lines of credit, none of which he tapped.

Although having access to these funds cost him more in terms of interest and ownership, J.C. considered it well worth the price. "It was like paying an insurance premium. It cost a bit more but provided a safety net. Money was one less thing I had to worry about," he says. "A lot of potentially good companies have died because they ran out of money. I looked at the things that could kill us, and I could control this one." Moreover, he avoided the constraints that often come with outside investors by setting clear expectations with his investor group. He promised them a healthy return on their money on the condition that they would have no control over how he developed and managed the venture.

Some entrepreneurs and academics warn against the dangers of overfunding an early-stage business, arguing that too much capital can cause an entrepreneur to lose touch with market forces or become inflexible or undisciplined. My experience is that these dangers operate independently of a venture's funding situation, biting poorly funded and well-funded businesses alike, and they are driven mostly by factors such as the founder's preparation, personality, and expertise. In J.C. Faulkner's case, the extra funding *heightened* his ability to focus and respond intelligently to market forces. "The fact that we had more money than we needed meant that we could go faster if we wanted, or we could slow things down," he said, "depending on what the markets were doing."

Bob Tucker, J.C. Faulkner's attorney, believes that the principle of ample funding generalizes well to the many business owners with whom he has worked over the years. "I have advised dozens of different businesses to go borrow money," he says. "If your business plan indicates you're going to need a good bit of money down the road, go right now, even if it costs you more in interest to do so, because you don't know what lies between here and there. It's worth having the powder in the keg, because the consequence of not borrowing now may be that your business plan won't get a chance because of future developments of some kind."

COMMIT RESOURCES WISELY

Raising ample funds is one side of the financial equation that will determine the length of your startup runway. The other is your burn rate, the negative cash flow likely to be created during your launch. As you build your venture with an eye toward managing risk, preserving flexibility, and staying in the game, your rate of spending will be a critical lever for extending and stretching your time and cash.

Don't confuse raising money with the need to spend it. Instill a disciplined process of managing your commitment of funds and monitoring projected cash levels. The more judiciously you manage expenses, the more you multiply the power and impact of whatever capital is available.

Mark Williams gives much credit for Modality's early staying power to the role of Nancy Owens, who first came on board in a part-time accounting and finance role but soon became his CFO and chief administrator. "Nancy, along with great financial advisers around us, helped us manage cash and operate with a high level of capital efficiency," he says. "You want to raise as much capital as you can, but you have to be extremely careful in how you utilize those resources."

Keep in mind that committing resources wisely is not the same thing as minimizing all costs. Once you have chosen the right starting point, you will enable your venture's growth by making targeted investments, not by completely avoiding them. Bob Tucker remembers that J.C. Faulkner's approach to spending money during D1's launch was well planned, focused, and confident. "Something that J.C. did that I believe is an earmark of success: Focus more on what you want to spend and what you want to spend it for, than on trying to curb the expense," he said. "In other words, make the expenditures well thought-out, prudent, and necessary in support of the business plan, as opposed to thinking 'let's save everything we can.' That's not your objective. Your objective is to enable and support the business plan."

A key factor determining where and how you commit your early-stage resources will be the pace with which you intend to launch and grow your venture. The right pace for your particular business will, in turn, be driven by many factors, including your purpose as an entrepreneur (*What pace will best align with your personal goals?*), the nature of your market opportunity (*How robust is market demand for your offering?*), related competitive forces (*Is your window of opportunity narrow or wide?*), and your business model and strategy (*What rate of growth will best position you to create value in proportion to the opportunity?*).

By mid-2010, Mark Williams and his team faced a set of divergent opportunities for growth. Their research and development efforts continued to generate potentially game-changing innovations for Apple's iPhone and iPad products, as well as enterprise-wide learning solutions for educational institutions, healthcare systems, and large corporations. Focusing on innovation would call for a deep investment of time and capital with uncertain returns. At the same time, Modality's steady investment in its catalog of licensed educational and reference products for mobile devices had led to a library of nearly 150 products and a reliable revenue stream. The company had also begun to generate fees for providing digital publishing services for major publishers. Each of these areas of opportunity brought a unique set of risks and requirements, and Mark and his team faced tough choices regarding where to invest limited resources.

As a general rule of thumb, I have found that most startup founders, driven by their enthusiasm and commitment, attempt to do too much, too fast. Successful entrepreneurs often look back on their path to value creation as less like a sprint than a marathon, one that balances urgency and desire with watchfulness, patience, and good judgment. As Amar Bhide, visiting scholar at Harvard University's Kennedy School of Government, wrote in his classic piece on bootstrap finance in the November-December 1992 *Harvard Business Review*, "Start-ups that failed because they could not fund their growth are legion. Successful bootstrappers take special care to expand only at the rate they can afford and control."[9]

Founder-Level Strategies: Performing and Persevering over Time

During 2008, as it became increasingly clear that the market for upscale adult daycare services in Charlotte was not going to materialize any time soon, Lynn Ivey continued to doggedly pursue her dream. She brought on a temporary sales team to generate and follow through on leads. She continued to network with enthusiasm throughout the community, seeking client referrals and new financial partners. But privately, Lynn wrestled with despair and depression. Fatigued by financial crises, she searched for pockets of cash and juggled vendor and bank payments to generate another month's payroll. It had been more than a year since her mother had passed away, and her lingering grief was now deepened by the growing realization that her business, a monument launched in her mother's memory, was itself in the process of dying.

The birth of a business idea brings hope, jubilation, and intensity. Aspiring entrepreneurs feed off of this energy and spread it to others as they race forward. Friends and colleagues admire and congratulate new founders on their bravery and creativity. But it is further along the venture road, beyond the honeymoon's promise, in times of strife and stress and inescapable responsibility, where many businesses are made or broken. Your entrepreneurial stamina and determination will occasionally seem like the only thread holding your venture together. In these times, the most vital questions have little to do with your business model and everything to do with you: *How much gas is left in your tank? How do you refuel and recover? Are you moving with enthusiasm and a sense of purpose or with growing weight on your shoulders?*

In this section, I will offer a few final thoughts on how to perform and persevere through good times and bad in pursuit of your venture-level goals. While we know that certain entrepreneurs are more hard-wired for persistence than others (see personality dimensions covered in Chapter Three), I will focus here on strategies available to all founders, regardless of core personality. Healthy entrepreneurial stamina is not just about the refusal to quit, an attitude that can cause stubbornness and attachment to nonviable concepts, but is grounded in ongoing learning and improvement. Four principles can help you to increase your own staying power for the good of yourself and your venture:

1. Feed your fire.

2. Focus on achievable goals.

3. Balance performance with recovery.

4. Persevere without attaching.

FEED YOUR FIRE

As a kid, I loved waking up to the sound of distant lawn mowers drifting through my window, a signal that the weekend had arrived. Saturdays were packed with possibility. I would hop out of bed and spend whole days in pursuit of activities of my own choosing, playing "homerun derby" with my buddies, teaching myself to high-jump at a nearby athletic field, or listening to my older brothers' record collections while studying album art and memorizing lyrics. Every few months, I rotated to a newly immersive activity. One season it was basketball, the next music, then reading, fishing, or golf. In every case, I loved what I was doing. I loved the exploration, the striving, and the opportunity to learn and master new things. Passion and joy drove me, not fear or obligation. I was free.

Forty years later, I still seek and enjoy that Saturday morning feeling, the "fire in the belly" that pulls me out of bed as I look forward to the activities of the day ahead. I seek it out in my relationships, in my work, and in my personal pursuits. I believe all of us yearn for the moments when we feel on course, called and driven by a sense of purpose, focused on what we are moving *toward* rather than what we are hoping to escape. This is the essence of entrepreneurial passion, a self-evident compulsion driven by instinct, needing no explanation.

Most of us, too, can identify with another feeling, more like a "weight on the shoulders," a feeling of resignation and compliance, of doing a job because we seem to have no choice. It's the hit-the-snooze-button syndrome, where we most look forward to the end of the day. When it comes to personal energy and stamina, the difference between these two states is like the difference between the Saturdays and Mondays of my youth.

A key strategy for building your own perseverance and performance as an entrepreneur is to know what activates the fire in your belly. As your startup road becomes more challenging: *Why do you continue to care? What are your compelling reasons for persevering? What is it about your business that most energizes you? In what ways are your expertise and passion best utilized?* On the other side of the coin: *What issues and activities provoke frustration or fear? Where are your feet stuck in mud because of a lack of desire, skill, or confidence? How can you better align the goals of your venture, and your role in leading it, with your natural motivation and capabilities?*

As I wrote in Chapter Three, *founder readiness* is more than a prelaunch issue. Your level of preparation and performance will continue to determine your venture's health long after the launch button is activated. To ensure the best fit between your role and the needs of your venture, periodically revisit the questions provided in Chapter Three related to your purpose and goals, skills and experience, relationships and resources, and personal capacity. *How are these factors playing out along your venture path? How can you maximize the fit and alignment between your goals, skills, and the needs for your new business?*

FOCUS ON ACHIEVABLE GOALS

One of the challenges for passionate founders with ambitious ideas is to not be overwhelmed and stymied by the size and complexity of the venture opportunity. The old axiom about how to eat an elephant—one bite at a time—will serve you well as you seek to accelerate down your startup runway. Break your grand vision into shorter-term, readily achievable goals to encourage clear progress and rapid iteration. From a motivational perspective, the achievement of each step brings its own psychological reward, a dose of satisfaction, and a sense that your venture is gaining ground.

In an article summarizing a longitudinal study of nascent entrepreneurs, Sibin Wu, Linda Matthews, and Grace Dagher of the University of Texas (Pan American) observe that achievement-oriented entrepreneurs tend to do best with a measured approach to goal setting. "For highly complex tasks, such as the entrepreneurial process, difficult goals are not as effective as simple goals," they write. "Entrepreneurs tend to be overconfident and overestimate their abilities and their business goals. They may overconfidently set their goals too high . . . and hence experience dissatisfaction instead of satisfaction."[10] It's important to emphasize here that setting achievable goals does *not* equate to shrinking from adversity or ignoring challenging tasks. The lesson is not to abandon your ultimate vision but to keep your eyes focused on the difficult but achievable steps that will get you there.

To boost the positive effect of your short-term goal setting, create regular points of accountability at which you will share results with others. Paul Graham, founder of Y Combinator, a seed-stage technology venture capital fund, has wryly observed that perhaps the biggest differentiator between successful and failing startup teams funded by Y Combinator is how consistently these founding teams attend Tuesday night dinners hosted by him and his colleagues. In a talk to his founders entitled "How Not to Die," Graham said, "You've probably noticed that having dinners every Tuesday with us and the other founders causes you to get more done than you would otherwise, because every dinner is a mini Demo Day. Every dinner is a kind of a deadline. So the mere constraint of staying in regular contact with us will push you to make things happen . . . It would be pretty cool if merely by staying in regular contact with us, you could get rich. It sounds crazy, but there's a good chance that would work."[11]

BALANCE PERFORMANCE WITH RECOVERY

Sustained, world-class performance in any field requires what Jim Loehr, renowned performance psychologist and co-founder of the Human Performance Institute, calls *oscillation,* the balancing of intense periods of focus and effort with intermittent periods of recovery and development. Over several decades, Dr. Loehr and his partners have closely examined the behavior of peak performers across sports, business, medicine, law enforcement, and other fields.[12] Virtuoso musicians, champion tennis players, and high-performing technologists all display a similar back-and-forth pattern of intense effort and recovery. The same is true of the best entrepreneurs. Any talented founder can run hard and bring his or her "A" game for a few weeks or a few months, but leaders who display strong venture leadership over the longer term find ways to care for themselves and their loved ones, recharge their batteries, and sharpen their skills and knowledge.

Sustaining your effectiveness as a founder will require punctuating your work with adequate time for recovery, practice, and play. A simple (but often ignored) example is in the area of self-care. Many frazzled entrepreneurs don't allow themselves enough sleep, exercise, or nutrition. They envision themselves as tough, stoic warriors, whereas, in fact, their health and intellect are fading fast. Personally, I have yet to find a more reliable way to replenish my strength, mind, and mood than to engage in regular exercise, but each founder will need to find his or her own rhythm and approach for staying sharp and increasing capacity.

If you don't take time for recovery, chances are good that your mind and body will do it for you. In early 2010, Mark Williams noticed that Modality's top software developer, a brilliant technologist and the indispensable backbone of the firm's innovation and development efforts, was not performing up to his own historical standards. The behavior was extremely uncharacteristic, and when Mark directly shared his concerns, he learned that his colleague was on the verge of burning out. "He said he had hit a wall, to the point where he hadn't wanted to look at another line of code," Mark said. "We encouraged him to take more personal downtime and he began to work his way back into a groove." Interestingly, Mark Williams himself, one of the most steadily energetic founders I've ever known, someone who could work for months on end with as little as four to five hours of sleep each night, seems to hit his own wall every six months or so, going down for days at a time with a severe intestinal bug or a high-fever strain of the flu.

Another form of this physical and emotional rebellion comes in the form of weak focus, wandering attention, and unclear thinking. It has become fashionable among entrepreneurs to claim to suffer from some version of Adult Attention Deficit Disorder, and no doubt some of us do, but most of us are victims of an unrelenting overload of sensory stimulation and emotional strain. Too many founders allow their focus to be diluted and washed away by incessant interruptions and distractions, whether they are by emails, advertisements, or random insignificant tasks.

Two books have recently contributed to the growing body of evidence that cultural and technological forces are shrinking our attention spans and diminishing our productivity and effectiveness. In *The Myth of Multitasking*, author and consultant Dave Crenshaw explains how the modern tendency to wear many hats and juggle tasks leads to huge drains on productivity and efficiency.[13] And in *The Shallows: What the Internet Is Doing to Our Brains*, journalist Nicholas Carr offers the well-formulated thesis that our 24/7 information age is robbing us of nothing less than our ability to think deeply.[14]

The solution is to prioritize and focus the largest chunks of your time on opportunities and problems that require deep attention and effort. Go for depth over breadth. Devote your best thinking and action to a few essential challenges each week, or even each month, to avoid being pulled by the tide of a hundred superficial distractions, drifting like a boat without a sail. Determine what initiatives are most essential to propel your venture forward over a given period of time, and then shut everything else out. Turn off the screens and get back to a college-ruled note pad if necessary.

PERSEVERE WITHOUT ATTACHING

The deepest form of entrepreneurial commitment acknowledges and accepts that there are forces in the marketplace that are beyond the founder's control, forces that will impact the venture's destiny for better or worse. Rather than causing a resilient founder to give up, this realization highlights for them the fact that every route to venture success will deviate in some way from early expectations. Persevering over time requires that the entrepreneur commit to the path forward without knowing exactly where it will lead.

On a bright spring morning at The Ivey in May of 2010, twenty elderly clients sat around a children's choir, visiting from a local middle school. Lynn Ivey's dog Lacy rested in the lap of a contented woman. Staff members tried to coax people to sing along, and many did. Others tapped a hand against a leg or a foot on the floor. Lynn noticed her grumpiest member, a man who usually protested every staff request, sitting with his eyes raised upward, smiling and singing to the lofted ceiling. Soon another more powerful voice began to lift above the crowd. Heads turned to see one of the center's newest members, a woman of stately bearing, standing on the outer edge of the group. This former professional opera singer had returned to her stage.

Six years after she left her bank job to care for her ailing mother, Lynn Ivey was beginning to taste her vision in real terms. This was the kind of personal impact she imagined: a home-away-from-home for people who desperately needed it, a community full of life, and a cast of characters bringing plenty of challenge and humor. Lynn couldn't help but smile in describing the staff member who raced to intercept a man trying to relieve himself in a trashcan or the pleasant woman who seemed to be an aspiring thief, slipping the occasional vase or photo frame into her purse on the way out the door.

The fact that Lynn Ivey has been able to keep the center operating into 2010 is a testament to the sheer power of her personal will. When asked about what has kept her going, she talked of several factors. "I've never been a person who gives up on things," she said. "I completely invested myself in this, financially, emotionally, and in every other way." She was also driven, she said, by the public visibility and her responsibility to deliver on her promise to The Ivey's many stakeholders. She credited her own spiritual outlook as well, a steadfast belief that something bigger was at work. And she still believed that The Ivey was on the front lines in an effort to address a growing societal problem. "A wave is coming," she said. "We are meeting a core need that will only continue to grow."

Just as critical for Lynn's survival to this point was her late-blooming ability to let go of cherished ideas. Chief among them was her belief that The Ivey could thrive as a for-profit business. In 2009 she came full circle, finally accepting an idea that a few colleagues had advocated early in her planning process: to operate as a nonprofit organization. As her funds had continued to dwindle, this became the best option for keeping her fledgling service alive. "We needed money, and we needed more clients," she says. "The nonprofit approach helped us make gains in both areas." It allowed her to begin raising funds in the form of charitable donations, still a challenging task in a tough economy but also a great fit for her skills, enthusiasm, and sense of vision. Operationally, the nonprofit status has allowed her to lower her fees and offer her services to a much wider audience. As a result, she had acquired forty full-time members by May of 2010, a number climbing steadily month after month.

Heading into the summer of 2010, great challenges remained for The Ivey. Lynn was increasingly focused on fund-raising opportunities and continued to think big, promoting a vision for extending her model to the national level. In June, she entertained a week-long visit from the founder of an upscale adult daycare center planned in the Pacific Northwest region of the United States. "You should see her business plan," Lynn said, "It's almost exactly like the one I wrote." Lynn was eager to share her lessons learned with this founder and continued to look for opportunities to forge mutually beneficial partnerships.

The only thing certain about The Ivey's future is that it would bring plenty of new and unpredictable hurdles. Lynn felt up to the challenge, encouraged by the people being served right in front of her.

She was beginning to make peace with the shape that her vision was taking. A few weeks after the middle school choir had visited her center, she told me of a brief conversation just after the choir had left the building. As she made her way back to her office in a hallway just off of the lobby, a frail eighty-year-old woman touched her elbow. "She said that she needed for me to know what a special place this was for her," Lynn remembered, "and how grateful she was to be here."

"I thought, in that moment," she finished, "that my mom was talking to me."

Startup Readiness Tool

This tool can be used to:

- Evaluate and improve a founding team's readiness to launch a business

- Calibrate the timing of a startup effort (accelerate or delay)

- Assess the growth potential of an already established venture

- Provoke honest conversations about priority issues among founders, partners, and investors

- Pinpoint areas where focused support will increase the probability of success

As a new or aspiring founder, you can dramatically improve your odds of success and happiness by evaluating and focusing on the right fundamentals early in your entrepreneurial journey. The questions in the following pages are the result of my twenty years of experience as an organizational consultant, entrepreneur, and investor. They are designed to help you assess your distinctive set of strengths, opportunities, and needs, and to identify your priorities going forward: What important decisions need to be made? What questions need further research and reflection? What actions must be taken? What issues must be addressed?

As you review the list of questions, take into account the following considerations:

- Answering these questions may require a good deal of your time and energy. Many tools for entrepreneurs have been reduced to "fast food" style checklists, but, when it comes to the fundamentals of startup success, there are no shortcuts. The goal is not to perfect or over-analyze your idea, but to systematically improve your likelihood of success by anticipating and addressing the domains known to impact success.

- Each founder, and each venture, is unique. Some of the questions will prove more relevant to your particular business and situation than others. Start with a quick review of all questions, flagging those that seem most timely and important based on your phase and situation. Then work through the questions you have flagged as most valuable, while being careful not to avoid questions simply because they are tough to answer, or make you uncomfortable.

- Some questions will require more data or more reflection, or may be unanswerable at your current phase. Work to gain clarity on these questions over time, and use this framework as a tool to continually reassess your venture's strengths and weaknesses as time passes.

- There are five sets of questions. The first is a set of *orienting* questions. The next four correspond to the four-quadrant framework for new venture success introduced in Chapter Six (*founder, market, math,* and *execution*), as seen in Figure A-1.

Figure A-1. Four-quadrant framework for new venture success.

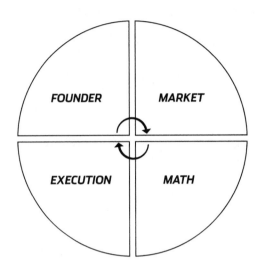

Orienting Questions

O1. Describe your *business concept* in fifty words or less: What will you offer? For whom? What about your idea is most compelling and unique?

O2. *How many founders* are currently involved? If only yourself, are you open to bringing co-founders on board, including giving up some ownership? Why or why not?

O3. What *other stakeholders / partners* are involved at this point? Should they provide input into this process?

O4. What is the *size and scale* of your envisioned business? Why?

O5. *How far along are you in pursuing the idea?*

- Contemplating / considering?
- Actively planning / researching?

- Developing the product or service?

- Product/service is ready to launch?

- Business is launched (pre-revenue)?

- Business is generating revenue?

- Business is profitable?

O6. *Current time allocation:* How many hours per week are you currently devoting to the development of your new venture? How many hours per week are you currently devoting to job(s) *other* than your new venture?.

Founder Questions

PURPOSE AND GOALS

F1. *Purpose:* Why are you pursuing this venture? (Review the reasons listed below and check those that most closely describe you and your venture. You might also note any that specifically do not apply to you. What are the predominant themes regarding your motivation and drive?)

Independence/Self-Reliance

- To work independently, call my own shots

- Set my own schedule, work at my own pace

- Freedom to set my own standards and priorities

Achievement

- To prove to myself I can do it/accomplish something challenging

- See a better way of doing something (or want to do work of higher quality)

- To stretch, learn, grow, get better
- To be the best at something/to compete successfully.

Lifestyle (to mesh with a desired lifestyle *outside* of work)

- To spend more time with family
- To support the non-work parts of my life
- To live the way I want *outside* of work

Higher Calling/Greater Good

- To help people
- To build something that outlasts me; leave a legacy
- More meaningful or fulfilling work
- To meet a need in society

Professional Advancement

- To take professional skills/contribution to a higher level
- To go more deeply into my specialty
- To develop an idea

Social/Community

- To work with friends
- To create a great place to work
- To be part of a great team
- To have fun, meet new people

An Escape from Something

- To get out of an unsatisfactory job
- To get away from a bad boss
- Feel bored, stagnant

- No good options right now in the job market

- Working for others no longer provides security

Financial/Wealth

- To increase my annual salary/earnings

- To create long-term wealth

Market Opportunity

- Driven by a great product/service idea

- Irresistible opportunity (a timely market or customer need)

- See a better solution for an existing problem

Creativity/Artistry

- Creative pursuits . . . to maximize my time creating something

- To develop new products or innovations

- To turn a passion into a job (hobby, skill, craft, etc.)

- To create something—the thrill of building something

Identity (It's Who I Am)

- I've always been an entrepreneur at heart

- To follow in parent's or family's footsteps

Situational

- Take advantage of a windfall financial gift

- Downsized or lost job

- Friend or colleague presented the opportunity

F2. *Goals:* What do you hope to achieve (personally and professionally) in the short-term (next 1–2 years) and longer-term (5+ years)?

F3. Describe your *desired lifestyle* as you move forward with your new business.

SKILLS AND EXPERIENCE

F4. Describe *any past entrepreneurial experience* starting up or running a business (as founder, as member of startup team, or launching business within a larger company). How do these experiences relate to your new business?

F5. What relevant *work experience and training* do you bring? What is your breadth and depth of experience in the venture's targeted *field or industry?*

F6. *Core skill set:* What do you know how to do at the highest level? What can you do better than most everyone else? How do these skills relate to your new business?

F7. What *supervisory, management, or leadership experience* do you bring? (Scope and scale of prior responsibilities, time served, etc.)

F8. What *sales and marketing experience* do you bring? What kind and for how long?

- Within targeted market/industry?

- Outside targeted market/industry?

F9. What *general business seasoning and work skills* do you bring within the following domains?

- Negotiation (contracts, deals, etc.)

- Organization, planning, project management

- Problem solving and decision making

- Financial acumen (financial reporting, accounting, etc.)

- Networking, developing business relationships

- Communication (written, oral)

- Public speaking

- Senior executive interaction

- Other (any skill or experience that you see as relevant)

F10. *Adversity.* What have been *your toughest challenges*, professionally or personally? How did you handle these experiences and what did you learn from them?

PERSONALITY, HEALTH, AND TRANSITION

F11. *Entrepreneurial Personality, Values, and Tendencies.* How strongly do you exhibit the characteristics in the list below? (For an empirically validated assessment of your entrepreneurial profile along these dimensions, visit www.ReadyFounder.com). How well does your personality match up with the demands of your startup process? What role(s) will allow to best utilize your strengths? How can you compensate in areas where your personality is not a great match for your venture's needs?

- *Commercially Oriented*—interested in money and business; driven to achieve bottom-line profitability.

- *Conceptual*—an "idea person," continually unearthing new opportunities; an *emergent learner*, adaptively learning from experience and experimentation; skillfully deals with ambiguity and complexity, and has the ability to discern useful patterns from large amounts of information.

- *Independent*—willing or inclined to strike out on your own; willing to stand apart from the herd.

- *Achievement Oriented*—passionate, ambitious, competitive, driven; enjoys mastering new skills, displays a strong work ethic, and sets high standards for themselves and others.

- *Risk Tolerant*—evaluates and manages calculated risks; shows courage in the face of uncertainty, and distinguishes internal feelings of anxiety from more objective measures of actual risk.

- *Confident*—understands own abilities and contribution (optimistic but realistic); not easily deterred by others' negativity or criticism.

- *Persuasive*—appeals to others' motives and values by tuning in to the needs and interests of others and adapting the message and behavior to match.

- *Resilient*—persistently works to overcome obstacles and does not allow setbacks to derail them; perseveres in the face of adversity.

- *Reliable/Focused*—follows through, delivering on commitments to others, as well as to themselves.

- *People Oriented*—values, understands, and leverages people; possesses strong social antennae; gifted at working a room and building lasting relationships.

- *Ethical*—holds self to high personal and professional standards. Words and actions are aligned; builds trust and credibility with customers, team members, and partners.

F12. What is the status of your *physical/emotional health?* How do you develop and maintain your *personal energy and capacity* (e.g., exercise, nutrition, social and spiritual, etc.)?

F13. *Transition:* What aspects of your prior roles and responsibilities do you want to carry forward into this new phase (will serve you well)? What aspects do you want to leave behind (will hinder you in some way)? These might include affiliations, contracts, responsibilities, behaviors, etc.

RELATIONSHIPS AND RESOURCES

F14. What *helpful relationships/contacts* do you bring, including potential:

- Clients/customers
- Team members or employees
- Mentors/advisers
- Service partners (legal, financial, HR, consulting)
- Suppliers
- Investors/funders
- Referral sources
- Other

F15. What *financial resources* are available to you (savings, ready investors, existing lines of credit, etc.)? Describe type and amount.

PERSONAL NEEDS AND INTERESTS

F16. What *minimum personal income* do you need to earn on a monthly basis over the next twelve to thirty-six months to be able to pursue this venture?

F17. What are your longer-term *personal financial goals* in pursuing this venture?

- Annual return beyond thirty-six months?
- Total personal return from business?

F18. What current commitments of your time (other than new venture) will remain in place? How many hours/weeks do you expect to spend on this venture?

FAMILY ALIGNMENT/SUPPORT

F19. Are family / significant others fully aware of what this venture will require?

F20. How *supportive* (confident, committed) are your family / significant others?

- Actively supportive (want to help, willing to sacrifice)?

- Supportive in principle?

- Neutral or mixed?

- Passively resistant (have concerns but won't stand in the way)?

- Actively resistant (might pose obstacles to progress)?

F21. *Who else* are you counting on to support this venture? What is their level of support or resistance?

Market Questions

M1. How do you define your market? What basic *need or problem* are you solving?

- What value will you create for customers?

- Are you solving an acute problem for customers, or providing a nice-to-have benefit?

- What customer pain are you addressing, directly or indirectly?

M2. Who is your *core customer?*

- Who is already using your product or service, or something like it? What's motivating them to use it?

- How would you describe those who are the best fit for

your products or services? Why are they a good fit?

- What is their financial/budget capacity?

- Who are potential "marquee" customers (major relationships that will put your business on the map and drive additional business)?

M3. What is the nature of your *market opportunity*?

- How large is the market? How fast is it growing (or declining)? Why is it growing (or declining)? Is it emerging or mature? Fragmenting or consolidating? What is most compelling about it?

- What's happening in your industry? What larger forces and trends are driving the opportunity (economic, technological, demographic, social, regulatory, environmental, etc.)?

- How long will your window of opportunity be open? Why is this the right time to enter the market (or if not now, when is the right time)?

- How broad or narrow is the market opportunity? What segments/niches/tiers will your business target?

- Other relevant market issues/questions to address?

M4. *What will be your approach* to marketing and selling your offering?

M5. Who is currently addressing (or attempting to address) the opportunity, and how? What are their strengths and weaknesses? Why do you think the opportunity is not yet fully exploited?

M6. What is your *competitive advantage*? Is it durable, sustainable? What is unique about your offering (your *"secret sauce"*)? What differentiates you in the eyes of clients?

M7. What are *regulatory/legal* concerns or opportunities regarding this market?

M8. What *fundamental assumptions* about the market opportunity are most critical to your success? How can you test these assumptions?

M9. What are your most *pressing questions* to answer regarding your targeted customers or the overall market opportunity?

Math Questions

MT1. Describe your *vision* and *business model* (including options under consideration).

MT2. How will you *produce and distribute* your product or service?

MT3. What *capabilities* will be required? (Consider technology, skills, processes, "know-how," etc.)

MT4. What capabilities/skills should you *own vs. outsource?* Why?

MT5. What *resources/investments* will be required toward what expected *revenues*, along what *timeline?* What are strengths/concerns with the *financial projections?*

MT6. What are *projected cash levels* (best-, mid-, worst-case) over time?

MT7. What are *key financial indicators* to measure and manage going forward?

MT8. What *financial controls/systems* are in place, or planned?

MT9. What are highest-probability/highest-impact *risks to the plan?* How will these be managed (preventive, contingent actions)?

MT10. Based on your financial picture and personal needs/goals, what *total startup funds* are necessary to get the business off the ground?

- Is this enough to cover startup costs in a *worst-case* scenario?

- Is this enough to cover your minimum *short-term income needs?*

MT11. How much of the required funds are *currently available* to you for your use? What shortfall exists, if any?

MT12. What are available or prospective *options for filling the funding gap?*

MT13. *What are your next steps* toward exploring and securing the right funding sources?

Execution Questions

CAPABILITIES/TALENT

E1. What *skills/expertise* (beyond yours or your team's) are *required* to accomplish your near-term and long-term objectives?

E2. What *talent and expertise are needed* to supplement your own? Where are your most *pressing talent gaps?* What is your planned approach for filling out your team?

E3. Do you have *specific candidates* in mind? Are they the best available? How are their skills complementary to yours?

E4. What *service partners* will be necessary and what are your best available options?

- Legal
- Accounting/Finance
- Technology
- Marketing/PR
- HR
- Other

TECHNOLOGY

E5. What *key processes and systems* are required to develop, sell and deliver your products/services?

E6. What is your *sourcing plan* for key processes and systems?

E7. What *partners* may be necessary to provide, build, or support them?

TEAMWORK

E8. Who are your *key relationships*, inside and outside your business—relationships that must work well for your business to thrive?

E9. Are team goals, roles, and accountabilities clear? How strong are *relationships, trust, chemistry?*

E10. What management practices (regular meetings, team-development processes, social events, etc.) are in place for *continual strengthening of the team?*

INTEGRITY OF COMMUNICATION

E11. How open are you to considering *new ideas or data* that might contradict your business plan? Who do you utilize as a neutral sounding board or *devil's advocate* (someone who won't sugarcoat an opinion and will push back on your thinking)?

E12. To what extent are *tough or awkward issues* raised and discussed among key players (versus feel-good conversations)? How are differences of opinion raised and resolved? How is *bad news* handled?

E13. How *open and transparent* is your business plan and operation for those who need to know (key partners, investors, team members, etc.)?

E14. What important issues seem *undiscussable?* Why?

ALIGNMENT

E15. *Motivational Alignment.* What are the most important interests/ goals of each key venture player (partner, team member, major customer, etc.)? How well do these align with the interests/goals of the business? Where is misalignment? What needs to be done to correct?

E16. *Capability Alignment.* Are the right people in the right roles? Are key players deployed in ways that capitalize on their strengths and cover for weaknesses? How might capabilities be better aligned?

E17. *Financial Alignment.* How do compensation arrangements incent key members and partners to give their all in support of the new venture's goals? In what ways can salary, commission, bonus, ownership, and benefits structures be tweaked to maximize alignment?

E18. *Time Alignment.* What are your (or founding team's) top priorities? How well does your use of time align with these priorities? Where is misalignment? How should your time be reallocated, and what obstacles must be removed for this to occur?

Resources and Readings

Thanks to Internet search technology and social media interconnectivity, answers to most entrepreneurial questions can be found with a few clicks. I have attempted to list sources beyond the usual suspects, organized by the four quadrants of *founder, market, math*, and *execution*, along with a *general* section at the end. For an expanded, updated list, see www.ReadyFounder.com.

FOUNDER

Chapter Three – Founder Readiness

Entrepreneur Core Characteristics Profile (ECCP). The ECCP is a psychological assessment tool designed to help aspiring and practicing entrepreneurs understand how their distinctive personality traits and tendencies match up with characteristics of the typically successful entrepreneur. See www.ReadyFounder.com for more information.

Dweck, Carol. *Mindset: The New Psychology of Success.* New York: Ballentine, 2006. Dweck emphasizes the power of honest self-appraisal and commitment to the continuous road to mastery.

Pink, Daniel. *Drive: The Surprising Truth About What Motivates Us.* New York: Penguin, 2009. A useful exploration of internal motivation (see pages 153–161 for "Nine Strategies for Awakening Your Motivation").

Cornwell, Jeff. *The Entrepreneurial Mind.* www.drjeffcornwall.com. Cornwell keeps a foot in both the academic and practical worlds and brings a first-hand understanding of the challenges and tradeoffs of a founding role.

Slim, Pamela. *Escape from Cubicle Nation.* New York: Portfolio, 2009. www.escapefromcubiclenation.com. Pam is the model for healthy entrepreneurial passion and has mastered the terrain of the founder's personal journey as well as anyone I know.

Livingston, Jessica. *Founders at Work: Stories of Startups' Early Days.* Berkeley, CA: Apress, 2007. A fascinating collection of extensive interviews with technology venture founders about their early-phase experiences.

MARKET

Chapter Four – The Pull of the Market

Thomson, David G. *Blueprint to a Billion: 7 Essentials to Achieve Exponential Growth.* Hoboken, NJ: John Wiley & Sons, 2006. Whether or not you are interested in growing a billion-dollar business, Thomson's research has isolated market-oriented growth principles that apply to all ventures. (See especially Chapters 3, 4, and 5.)

Terwiesch, Christian, and Karl Ulrich. *Innovation Tournaments: Creating and Selecting Exceptional Opportunities.* www.innovationtournaments.com. The authors outline an intriguing process for vetting ideas and opportunities in a competitive free-market framework.

Sull, Donald N. "Strategy as Active Waiting." *Harvard Business Review*, September 2005. In this article, Sull provides insights and tactics for monitoring and responding to market forces, including scanning for market "anomalies."

Seth Godin Blog, The. http://sethgodin.typepad.com. Also check out Godin's book, *The Dip* (New York: Portfolio, 2007), for a quick, useful immersion into the question of when to stay the course or change direction.

Steven Blank Blog, The. http://steveblank.com. I think of Steve Blank as the godfather of market focus. His first book, *The Four Steps to the Epiphany* (San Mateo, CA: Cafepress, 2005), is not for the casual reader, but it introduced the groundbreaking notion of "customer development" (vs. product development).

Ries, Eric. "The Five Whys for Start-Ups." *Harvard Business Review*, http://blogs.hbr.org/cs/2010/04/the_five_whys_for_startups.html. Borrowing from lean manufacturing techniques, Ries illustrates a simple, powerful tool for fixing the root causes of business problems.

MATH

Chapter Five – Your Math Story

Berry, Tim. *The Plan-as-You-Go Business Plan.* Irvine, CA: Entrepreneur Press, 2008. A flexible, commonsense approach to planning from a planning guru. Favorite quote: "If you dread planning your startup, don't start it."

Osterwalder, Alexander, and Yves Pigneur. *Business Model Generation.* Hoboken, NJ: John Wiley & Sons, 2010. The definitive framework for getting clear on what you are attempting to do with your venture.

Buffett, Warren E. Berkshire Hathaway, Inc., *Chairman's Letters to Shareholders* (1977–2009), http://www.berkshirehathaway.com/letters/letters.html. Although Buffett is famous for proclaiming "we don't do startups," the fundamental business logic represented in more than two decades of his letters to Berkshire Hathaway shareholders is invaluable for any aspiring entrepreneur who wants to ground a business model in proven fundamentals of venture success.

Reiss, Bob, and Jeffrey L. Cruikshank. *Low Risk, High Reward: Practical Prescriptions for Starting and Growing Your Business.* New York: The Free Press, 2000. Bob Reiss is a timeless entrepreneur, whose insights apply across new and old school industries. Chapter 2, on *numeracy,* and Chapter 3, on *managing risk,* will help you develop a clear, compelling math story.

Wilson, Fred. http://www.avc.com. The principal of Union Square Ventures, offers a refreshing take on VC funding issues and opportunities.

Charan, Ram, and Noel M. Tichy. *Every Business Is a Growth Business.* New York: Three Rivers Press, 1998. Insight into universal market principles that endure over time and apply across industries. Charan and Tichy outline simple, powerful ways of thinking about growth and return. (See especially Chapter 3.)

Graham, Paul. *A Fundraising Survival Guide* (Essay). http://www.paulgraham.com/fundraising.html. A humorous, unvarnished look at the rigors of raising money, with tips on bootstrapping.

The Angel Capital Association. http://www.angelcapitalassociation.org/.

Venture Beat. www.venturebeat.com.

EXECUTION

Chapter Six – Startup Agility

Sull, Donald N. *The Upside of Turbulence: Seizing Opportunity in an Uncertain World.* New York: Harper Collins, 2009, and www.donaldsull.com. Sull is one of my favorite thinkers and strategists. His work on the nature of managerial commitments directly translates to tough choices facing new founders.

Ries, Eric. www.startuplessonslearned.com. Eric Ries has led a revolutionary wave of work on the concept of "the lean startup." Another technology-oriented entrepreneur and thought leader whose ideas apply to new ventures of all types and sizes.

Ries, Eric. "The Five Whys for Start-Ups." *Harvard Business Review,* http://blogs.hbr.org/cs/2010/04/the_five_whys_for_startups.html. Borrowing from lean manufacturing techniques, Ries illustrates a simple, powerful tool for fixing the root causes of business problems.

Senge, Peter, Art Kleiner, Charlotte Roberts, Richard Ross, and Bryan Smith. *The Fifth Discipline Fieldbook.* New York: Doubleday, 1994. A treasure trove of ideas and tools for learning and mastery in team and organizational contexts. (See "the wheel of learning," "systems thinking," and "team learning" concepts for agility- and learning-oriented content.)

Spear, Steven J. *The High-Velocity Edge: How Market Leaders Leverage Operational Excellence to Beat the Competition.* New York: McGraw-Hill, 2009. Spear is a talented thinker and writer whose work is all about problem-solving speed, continuous improvement, and how to leverage mistakes and "not knowing" for high performance.

After Action Review Process (AAR). http://www.fireleadership.gov/toolbox/after_action_review/aar.pdf. Originated in the U.S. Army and now widely used to incorporate lessons from any event into an ongoing cycle of learning.

Chapter Seven – Integrity of Communication

Heath, Chip, and Dan Heath. *Made to Stick: Why Some Ideas Survive and Others Die.* New York: Random House, 2007. An instant classic on how to ensure that your ideas cut through the clutter of the information age.

Collins, Jim. *Good to Great: Why Some Companies Make the Leap . . . and Others Don't.* New York: Harper Collins, 2001 and www.jim collins.com. Collins has made many contributions to leadership and organizational excellence. Most relevant here are his ideas on the value of "confronting the brutal facts."

Tedlow, Richard S. *Denial: Why Business Leaders Fail to Look Facts in the Face—and What to Do About It.* New York: Portfolio, 2010. Tedlow explores how denial trips up many over-optimistic entrepreneurs in this classic book.

Finkelstein, Sydney, Jo Whitehead, and Andrew Campbell. *Think Again: Why Good Leaders Make Bad Decisions and How to Keep it from Happening to You.* Boston: Harvard Business Press, 2008. The authors provide cases and anecdotes confirming the powerful effect of cognitive and emotional biases in human decision-making.

Macher, Ken. http://www.managementadvances.com. Ken Macher is one of the best at teaching venture teams to talk skillfully about their most critical issues.

Senge, Peter, et al. *The Fifth Discipline Fieldbook.* New York: Doubleday, 1994. This work deserves another mention for its section on "mental models," outlining several powerful tools for talking skillfully about things that matter most.

Scott, Susan. *Fierce Conversations: Achieving Success at Work and in Life One Conversation at a Time.* New York: Berkley Publishing Group, 2002. A simple, powerful set of tools and approaches for ensuring that communication is a competitive advantage in your venture team.

Chapter Eight – Staying Power

Crenshaw, Dave. *The Myth of Multitasking: How Doing It All Gets Nothing Done*. San Francisco: Jossey-Bass, 2008.

Human Performance Institute. http://hpinstitute.com/index.html. Training programs and tools for gaining and managing energy for the challenges of building a business over time. Founded by Jim Loehr (see below).

Loehr, Jim, and Tony Schwartz. *The Power of Full Engagement: Managing Energy, Not Time, Is the Key to High Performance and Personal Renewal*. New York: The Free Press, 2003. A full treatment of the concepts first offered in the Loehr and Schwartz article "The Corporate Athlete" (*Harvard Business Review*, January 2001).

Stallard, Michael. *Fired Up or Burned Out: How to Reignite Your Team's Passion, Creativity, and Productivity*. Nashville: Thomas Nelson, 2007. Emphasizes the importance of a "connection culture" in building sustainable performance and resilience among any team or workplace.

GENERAL

For basic checklists and tools for getting started, see www.inc.com and www.entrepreneur.com.

Ready Founder Services. www.readyfounder.com. Provides a framework and tools for evaluating and improving a venture idea, or for elevating the performance of an already existing business.

Women Entrepreneur. http://www.womenentrepreneur.com/. Full slate of content, tools, and advice for aspiring women entrepreneurs from publishers of *Entrepreneur* magazine.

Leonard, George. *Mastery: The Keys to Success and Long-Term Fulfillment.* New York: Penguin, 1992. This brief gem of a book will reward anyone interested in timeless and practical insights into how to achieve and sustain high performance.

Bygrave, William, and Andrew Zacharakis. *Entrepreneurship.* Hoboken, NJ: John Wiley & Sons, 2008. A soup-to-nuts tour of the entrepreneurial process that blends academic findings with accessible cases and practical tools.

Kawasaki, Guy. *The Art of the Start.* New York: Portfolio, 2004. Helpful advice from a serial entrepreneur/guru and digital age connector.

Harvard Business Review on Entrepreneurship (Harvard Business Review Paperback Series). This compendium is a bit dated (most articles were written in the 1990s), but Amar Bhide's featured pieces are timeless, capturing key issues and approaches for launching and managing new ventures.

Graham, Paul. www.paulgraham.com. Any time digesting Graham's essays is time well spent for an aspiring founder. A hacker at heart with universal appeal.

Drucker, Peter, *Innovation and Entrepreneurship.* New York: Harper & Row, 1985. Written in 1985 when the Internet was still a seed, so Drucker's wisdom must be filtered to apply in the digital age. But his core tenets continue to resonate.

SCORE: Counselors to America's Small Business. http://www.score.org/index.html.

Small Business Administration (SBA). http://www.sba.gov/.

Kauffman Foundation, The. http://www.kauffman.org/.

Notes

Chapter One – True Believers

1. Dave McClure, *Master of 500 Hats*. http://500hats.typepad.com.

2. Dan Bricklin, "Natural-born Entrepreneur," *Harvard Business Review* 79, no. 8 (September 2001): 54.

3. Pino G. Audia and Christopher I. Rider, "A Garage and an Idea: What More Does an Entrepreneur Need?" *California Management Review* 48, no. 1 (Fall 2005): 7.

4. David Whyte, *The Heart Aroused: Poetry and Preservation of the Soul in Corporate America* (New York: Doubleday, 1994), 78.

5. J.C. Faulkner's trusting relationship with Doug Crisp paid additional dividends for his startup business. A few months after J.C. left First Union to launch Decision One Mortgage, Doug Crisp decided to leave his senior executive role with the bank to join Decision One's management team. As director of operations, Doug played a major role in building and coordinating the talent, systems, and processes necessary to support the company's rapid growth.

6. Sam Harris, Sameer A. Sheth, and Mark S. Cohen, "Functional Neuroimaging of Belief, Disbelief, and Uncertainty," *Annals of Neurology* 63, no. 2 (February 2008): 141-147.

7. Andrew Newberg and Mark Robert Waldman, "Nuns, Buddhists, and the Reality of Spiritual Beliefs," in *Why We Believe What We Believe: Uncovering Our Biological Need for Meaning, Spirituality, and Truth* (New York: Free Press, 2006), 175.

8. Donna Marie De Carlos and Patrick Saparito, "Social Capital, Cognition, and Entrepreneurial Opportunities: A Theoretical Framework," *Entrepreneurship, Theory and Practice* 30, no. 1 (January 2006): 41-56.

9. Bella M. DePaulo and Kathy L. Bell, "Truth and Investment: Lies Are Told to People Who Care," *Journal of Personality and Social Psychology* 71, no. 4 (1996): 703-716.

10. Joseph Campbell, *The Power of Myth* (New York: Doubleday, 1988), 113.

11. This phrase is thought to be a paraphrasing of Goethe by W. H. Murray in *The Scottish Himalaya Expedition*, 1951. Murray's paraphrasing of Goethe is believed to come from a loose translation of *Faust* by John Anster in 1835.

Chapter Two – The Passion Trap

1. Guy Kawasaki, *The Art of the Start: The Time-Tested, Battle-Hardened Guide for Anyone Starting Anything* (New York: Portfolio, 2004).

2. Keith Hmieleski and Robert Baron, "Entrepreneur's Optimism and New Venture Performance: A Social Cognitive Perspective," *Academy of Management Journal* 32, no. 3 (2009): 475.

3. Ibid, 473-488.

4. Jay Goltz, *You're the Boss,* http://boss.blogs.nytimes.com/author/jay-goltz/.

5. Jeff Cornwall, *The Entrepreneurial Mind,* http://www.drjeffcornwall.com/.

6. John Osher, *17 Mistakes Start-Ups Make,* http://www.cpd.ogi.edu/MST/capstone/17Mistakes.htm.

7. Andy Herzfeld, "Reality Distortion Field," written February 1981, http://folklore.org/StoryView.py?project=Macintosh& story=Reality_Distortion_Field.txt&sortOrder=Sort%20by%20 Date&detail=medium&search=reality%20distortion%20field.

8. Colin Barker, *NeXT Computer: When Cool Wasn't Enough,* http://www.v3.co.uk/vnunet/features/2129861/computer-cool wasn-enough.

9. Sydney Finkelstein, Jo Whitehead, and Andrew Campbell, *Think Again: Why Good Leaders Make Bad Decisions and How to Keep It from Happening to You* (Boston: Harvard Business School Press, 2009).

10. Donna Marie De Carlos and Patrick Saparito, "Social Capital, Cognition, and Entrepreneurial Opportunities: A Theoretical Framework," *Entrepreneurship, Theory, and Practice* 30, no. 1 (January 2006): 41-56.

11. Mark Simon, Susan M. Houghton, and K. Aquino, "Cognitive Biases, Risk Perception, and Venture Formation: How Individuals Decide to Start Companies," *Journal of Business Venturing* 15, no. 2 (2000): 113-134.

12. Dan Lovallo and Daniel Kahneman, "Delusions of Success: How Optimism Undermines Executives' Decisions," *Harvard Business Review* 81, no. 7 (July 2003): 58.

13. Paul Graham, "Why Smart People Have Bad Ideas," *Paul Graham.com,* April 2005, http://www.paulgraham.com/bronze .html.

14. Hmieleski and Baron, "Entrepreneur's Optimism and New Venture Performance: A Social Cognitive Perspective," 475.

15. Mathew Hayward, Dean Shepherd, and Dale Griffin, "A Hubris Theory of Entrepreneurship," *Management Science* 52, no. 2 (2006): 160-172.

Chapter Three – Founder Readiness

1. Scott A. Shane, *The Illusions of Entrepreneurship: The Costly Myths That Entrepreneurs, Investors and Policy Makers Live By* (New Haven: Yale University Press, 2008), 98.

2. Ibid, 101.

3. Ibid, 117.

4. Vivek Wadhwa, Raj Aggarwal, Krisztina Holly, and Alex Salkever, "The Anatomy of an Entrepreneur: Family Background and Motivation," *Kauffman Foundation* (2009): http://www.kauffman.org/uploadedFiles/ResearchAndPolicy/TheStudyOfEntrepreneurship/Anatomy of Entre 071309_FINAL.pdf.

5. Matt Sussman, *Blogging Revenues, Brands and Blogs: SOTB 2009*, http://technorati.com/blogging/article/day-4-blogging-revenues-brands-and/.

6. Timothy Ferris, *The 4-Hour Workweek: Escape 9-5, Live Anywhere and Join the New Rich* (New York: Random House, 2007).

7. This entrepreneurial profile was developed through the author's collaboration with Adam Ortiz, Psy.D., of Executive Development Consulting, and Dr. S. Bartholomew Craig, of North Carolina State University.

8. Vivek Wadhwa, Richard Freeman, and Ben Rissing, "Education and Tech Entrepreneurship," *Kauffman Foundation* (2008): http://www.kauffman.org/uploadedfiles/Education_Tech_Ent_061108.pdf.

9. Ibid, 2.

10. A. H. Maslow, "The Theory of Human Motivation," *Psychology Review* 50, no. 4 (July 1943): 370-396.

11. Tim Berry, "5 Entrepreneurship Basics B-schools Don't Teach," written November 2009, http://timberry.bplans.com/2009/11/5-entrepreneurship-basics-b-schools-dont-teach.html.

12. Paul Graham, "18 Mistakes That Kill Startups," *PaulGraham.com*, October 2006, http://paulgraham.com/startupmistakes.html.

13. Jim Loehr and Tony Schwartz, "The Making of a Corporate Athlete," *Harvard Business Review* 79 no. 1 (2001): 120-128.

14. Jim Loehr and Tony Schwartz, *The Power of Full Engagement: Managing Energy, Not Time, Is the Key to High Performance and Personal Renewal* (New York: The Free Press, 2003).

15. William Bridges, *Transitions: Making Sense of Life's Changes* (Cambridge: De Capo Press, 2004).

16. Pamela Slim, *Escape from Cubicle Nation: From Corporate Prisoner to Thriving Entrepreneur* (New York: Portfolio, 2009).

17. Karlfried Von Durkheim, *The Way of Transformation: Daily Life as Spiritual Exercise* (London: Allen & Unwin, 1988).

Chapter Four – The Pull of the Market

1. John Heilemann, "Reinventing the Wheel," *Time*, December 2, 2001, http://www.time.com/time/business/article/0,8599,186 660,00.html.

2. Mark Gimein, "Reinventing the Wheel, Slowly," *BusinessWeek*, September 11, 2006, http://www.businessweek.com/magazine/ content/06_37/b4000411.htm?chan=tc&campaign_id=bier_ innstp.

3. Ibid.

4. Ibid.

5. William Bygrave and Andrew Zacharakis, *Entrepreneurship* (Hoboken: John Wiley & Sons, 2008), 101.

6. Paul Graham, "Why Smart People Have Bad Ideas," *PaulGraham.com*, April 2005, http://www.paulgraham.com/ bronze.html.

7. Blackfriars Communications, Inc., "Marketing 2005: Sizing US Marketing," written June 2005, http://www.researchandmarkets.com/reportinfo.asp?report_id=301653&t=d&cat_id=.

8. Seth Godin, *All Marketers Are Liars: The Power of Telling Authentic Stories in a Low-Trust World* (New York: Portfolio, 2005).

9. Bygrave and Zacharakis, *Entrepreneurship*, 167.

10. Joel Kurtzman, *Startups That Work* (New York: Portfolio, 2005), 31.

11. Jan Carlzon, *Moments of Truth* (Pensacola: Ballinger, 1987), 3.

12. David Thompson, *Blueprint to a Billion: 7 Essentials to Achieve Exponential Growth* (Hoboken: John Wiley & Sons, 2006).

13. Fred Jacobs, "Fly-In," written December 15, 2009, http://jacobs media.typepad.com/4sight/2009/12/flyin.html.

14. Get It Started: Wharton's Entrepreneurial Programs, "Segway's Dilemma," April 2008, http://wep.wharton.upenn.edu/gis/article.aspx?gisID=64.

Chapter Five – Your Math Story

1. Jan Brinckmann, Dietmar Grichnik, and Diana Kapsa, "Should Entrepreneurs Plan or Just Storm the Castle? A Meta-analysis on Contextual Factors Impacting the Business Planning–Performance Relationship in Small Firms," *Journal of Business Venturing* 25, no. 1 (2010): 24-40.

2. Amar Bhide, "How Entrepreneurs Craft Strategies That Work," *Harvard Business Review*, March-April 1994.

3. Tim Berry, *The Plan-As-You-Go Business Plan* (Irvine, CA: Entrepreneur Press, 2008).

4. Jeff Howe, *Crowdsourcing* (New York: Three Rivers Press, 2008).

5. Bob Reiss, with Jeffrey L. Cruikshank, *Low Risk, High Reward: Starting and Growing Your Business with Minimal Risk* (New York: The Free Press, 2000).

6. Ram Charan and Noel M. Tichy, *Every Business Is a Growth Business* (New York: Three Rivers Press, 1998), 48.

7. Joel Kurtzman, with Glenn Rifkin, *Startups That Work: The 10 Critical Factors That Will Make or Break a New Company* (New York: Portfolio, 2005).

8. Reiss with Cruikshank, 47.

9. Paul Hawken, *Growing a Business* (New York: Fireside, 1987), 126.

10. Scott A. Shane, *The Illusions of Entrepreneurship: The Costly Myths That Entrepreneurs, Investors, and Policy Makers Live By* (New Haven: Yale University Press, 2008), 117.

Chapter Six – Startup Agility

1. IBM Global Enterprise Services, "The Enterprise of the Future: IBM Global CEO Study" (Somers, NY: IBM, 2008).

2. Donald Sull, "Strategy as Active Waiting," *Harvard Business Review* (September 2005): 3.

3. More information about the Innovation Institute can be found at www.innovationatmccoll.org.

4. Eric Ries, "Don't Be the Ice Cream Glove," *Lessons Learned,* September 3, 2009, http://www.startuplessonslearned.com.

5. Maria Puente, "Snuggie Gets a Warm Embrace from Pop Culture," *USA Today.com,* January 27, 2009, www.usatoday.com.

6. Ries, "Don't Be the Ice Cream Glove."

7. Ibid.

8. Ibid.

9. Eric Ries, "The Engineering Manager's Lament," *Lessons Learned*, October 20, 2008, http://www.startuplessonslearned.com.

10. Eric Ries, "Case Study: Using an LOI to Get Customer Feedback on a Minimum Viable Product," *Lessons Learned*, October 23, 2009, http://www.startuplessonslearned.com.

11. Donald Sull, "Competing Through Organization Agility," *McKinsey Quarterly* no. 1 (2010): 49.

12. Arthur Rock, "Strategy vs. Tactics from a Venture Capitalist," *Harvard Business Review* 65 no. 6 (1987): 64.

Chapter Seven – Integrity of Communication

1. The Left-Hand Column technique was developed by Chris Argyris and Don Schon many decades ago to help people identify and understand the unspoken components underlying conversation, relationships, and learning processes. For more information see Peter Senge's *The Fifth Discipline Fieldbook*, pp. 246-252.

2. Howard Schultz, *Pour Your Heart into It: How Starbucks Built a Company One Cup at a Time* (New York: Hyperion, 1997), 80.

3. Paul Graham, "The Hardest Lessons for Startups to Learn," *PaulGraham.com*, April 2006, http://www.paulgraham.com/startuplessons.html.

4. John M. Darley and C. Daniel Batson, "From Jerusalem to Jericho: A Study of Situational and Dispositional Variables in Helping Behavior," *Journal of Personality and Social Psychology*, no 27 (July 1973): 100-108.

5. Michael S. Malone, "John Doerr's Startup Manual: Interview with John Doerr." *Fast Company*, February 28, 1997, http://www.fastcompany.com/magazine/07/082doerr.html.

6. Daniel Isenberg, "The Danger of Entrepreneurial Passion," *Harvard Business Review,* January 6, 2010, http://blogs.hbr.org/cs/2010/01/the_danger_of_entrepreneurial.html.

7. Alex Crippen, "Timeless and Time-Tested Warren Buffett Watch Predictions." *CNBC,* November 30, 2009, http://www.cnbc.com/id/34206949/Timeless_and_Time_Tested_Warren_Buffett_Watch_Predictions.

8. I borrow the terms *advocacy* and *inquiry* from Peter Senge and his many colleagues, who, in *The Fifth Discipline Fieldbook* and elsewhere, provide a set of indispensable concepts and tools for building learning organizations and practicing skillful conversations. (See Appendix B for more information.)

9. Jim Collins, "Hitting the Wall: Realizing That Vertical Limits Aren't," *JimCollins.com,* September 2003, http://www.jimcollins.com/article_topics/articles/hitting-the-wall.html.

10. Lloyd Albert Johnson, *A Toolbox for Humanity: More Than 9000 Years of Thought* (Victoria, Canada: Trafford, 2003), 97.

11. John Osher, *17 Mistakes Startups Make,* http://www.cpd.ogi.edu/MST/capstone/17Mistakes.htm.

12. Warren Buffett, "Chairman's Letter: Berkshire Hathaway, Inc., 2007 Annual Report" (2008): 7.

13. Jim Collins, *Good to Great: Why Some Companies Make the Leap... and Others Don't* (New York: HarperCollins, 2001), 85.

14. Vaclav Havel. Quoted in Amnesty International's essay "From Prisoner to President—A Tribute," 2003.

Chapter Eight – Staying Power

1. Scott A. Shane, *The Illusions of Entrepreneurship: The Costly Myths That Entrepreneurs, Investors, and Policy Makers Live By* (New Haven: Yale University Press, 2008), p.112.

2. "Accidental Entrepreneur," *Bloomberg BusinessWeek,* http://im ages.businessweek.com/ss/08/05/0512_accidental_entp/source /7.htm.

3. One of these two clients was Decision One Mortgage (D1), used as a case throughout this book. D1 not only became my favorite client over the next ten years, but the experience of working closely with J.C. Faulkner and his venture led me to commit to an extended study of entrepreneurial success, a path that led me eventually to the writing of this book.

4. Clark G. Gilbert and Matthew Eyring, "Beating the Odds When You Launch a New Venture," *Harvard Business Review* 88, no. 5 (May 2010): 92-98; "Dell Computer Corporation," *McGraw Hill Higher Education,* http://www.mhhe.com/business/management/ thompson/11e/case/dell5.html.

5. "Dell," *Innovate,* January-February 2006, http://www.innovation quotient.com/index.php?option=com_magazine&task=show_m agazine_article&magazine_id=21&Itemid=28&cat_id=3.

6. Mark Williams, e-mail message to author, February 21, 2007.

7. Gilbert and Eyring, "Beating the Odds," 95.

8. Ibid., 96.

9. Amar Bhide, "Bootstrap Finance: The Art of Start-Ups," *Harvard Business Review* 70, no. 6 (November-December 1992): 109-117.

10. Sibin Wu, Linda Matthews, and Grace K. Dagher, "Need for Achievment, Business Goals, and Entrepreneurial Persistence," *Management Research News* 30, no. 12 (2007): 937

11. Paul Graham, "How Not to Die," *Paul Graham.com,* August 2007, http://www.paulgraham.com/die.html.

12. Jim Loehr and Tony Schwartz, *The Power of Full Engagement: Managing Energy, Not Time, Is the Key to High Performance and Personal Renewal* (New York: The Free Press, 2003).

13. Dave Crenshaw, *The Myth of Multitasking: How Do It All Gets Nothing Done* (San Francisco: Jossey-Bass, 2008).

14. Nicholas Carr, *The Shallows: What the Internet Is Doing to Our Brains* (New York: W. W. Norton, 2010).

Index